C000257641

FAVOURITE
HOLY

Favourite Heroes and Holy People

CHOSEN BY PEOPLE FROM ALL WALKS OF LIFE

Compiled by
Deborah Cassidi

WITH WOOD ENGRAVINGS BY
A. J. CUNDALL

continuum

Continuum

The Tower Building, 11 York Road, London SE1 7NX

80 Maiden Lane, Suite 704, New York NY 10038

www.continuumbooks.com

First published 2008

British Library Cataloguing-in-Publication Data
A catalogue record for this book is available from the British Library.

ISBN: 978-1847-063-298

Library of Congress Cataloging-in-Publication Data
A catalog record for this book is available from the Library of Congress

Designed and typeset by Kenneth Burnley, Wirral, Cheshire
Printed and bound in Great Britain by MPG Books, Cornwall

*To my husband who has lovingly kept our ship afloat,
and to all my family for the joy they give.*

My thanks to the many generous contributors and copyright holders, to Jackie Cundall for the wood engravings and to my long-suffering family and friends; also to Marie and Mareile and in particular to Jane, Maggie, Laura, Philippa, Chris and Jeremy in the Somerset County Council Library Service. This book would not have been possible without their help.

Contents

Foreword

To make a collection of the words which keep us going, which shows up our individual reliance on a special poem or hymn or scrap of philosophy: could there be a more original example of the anthologist's art? Deborah Cassidi has succeeded in persuading an extraordinary range of people – men, women and, quite wonderfully, children – to allow her to publish the few words which they have found to make sense of life to them: witty words, profound words, sometimes quite ordinary words, most often perfectly expressed words. The net result is one of literate exposure. A grand language rides side by side with the simplest of language, a learned text with some popular rhyme.

While a few contributors rely on some safe old words about courage, the majority are simply amazing in the sheer variety of their hitherto secret mantras, until they were persuaded to send them for this enchanting collection. Some of us have a silent prayer, some of us a verse or two, some a saying which we may use as often as once a day to keep us going. The most innocent of things have been found to work. An editor might expect a quote from Plato, but the clear essence of this book is its truthfulness: its contributors have not searched around for impressive words which will look well under their names, but have told the rest of us those which, for reasons most of them are unable to explain, have hung around in their hearts. The result is moving, entertaining and marvellously readable. These pages are a brave confessional, the giving to the reader of a private wealth. Here the spirituality of the twentieth century rises above its unique evil through the words of its martyrs and writers.

There is a mine of mostly unfamiliar quotes from which to 'grow', on which to rely: it is a great read. Perhaps it is an instruction-book on how to be sensible and happy, selfless and inwardly quiet. Life, generally, is a wayward business, and here are a few thoughts to keep it in line. The great literary saints – Julian of Norwich with William Tyndale, Hildegard von Bingen and Traherne – good-naturedly share the text with Batman, Douglas Adams and Sir Humphrey; national heroes with non-heroes; priests with novelists, soldiers and sailors. Boys and girls write like angels. Many of the contributions have a way of disturbing the long-held notion of some public figure, and the general effect of that work is one of revelation.

This is a book to place alongside Lord Wavell's *Other Men's Flowers*, and is an anthology which acts as a corrective to many of today's statements on life. Suffering plays its bitter role in it, but what sustains its contributors, in the language used, is, for us, strengthening and worth sharing.

Ronald Blythe

The Threshold Prize is a tremendous encouragement to children's writing, with splendid results throughout Somerset. It has been well supported by two interesting anthologies, which have been widely enjoyed, and I am now delighted to commend the third, with the theme of *Favourite Heroes and Holy People*. This again has a varied range of fascinating contributions, from people of all ages, interests and experience. Not only is it a pleasure to read and reflect on, but it leads to a desire to know more about the subjects, with endless possibilities for even greater enjoyment and interest.

Elizabeth Acland Hood Gass
Lord-Lieutenant of Somerset

The Making of the Anthology

Compiling this third 'Favourites' anthology has been a journey threaded with gratitude, amazement and humility: gratitude to the contributors; amazement at the breadth of their choice of heroes, heroines and holy people (who I must collectively think of simply as 'heroes'); and humility before the sanctity and greatness of spirit of those admired people within these pages.

The book has been made by the contributors, and I thank them with all my heart. Many of them have turned out their libraries, their memories and their inner thoughts for a third time: the newcomers have been thrown in at the deep end.

I set them the difficult task of choosing not only a favourite hero or saint (and that 'saint' rapidly became a 'holy person'), but also of sending a quotation by or about that person. They responded in spades: and I ask for their indulgence for any crimes of omission or commission that I may have committed.

Some editing and shortening was necessary if the book was to stand any chance of being portable, so I often had to remind myself of Lord Menuhin's magnanimity when he sent a swathe of his personal philosophy for *Favourite Prayers* with the comment, 'Take any of it, all of it or none of it according to what suits the book.' So, like an interfering nanny, I reduced some of the paeans of praise and let the words and actions of the heroes stand more on their own merits.

The contributions are arranged mainly in alphabetical order of the contributor's name, but sometimes, where the same hero has been chosen, I have grouped them on the same page. The children's work is only roughly in alphabetical order as I have moved them a little to place them where they sit more comfortably or where the reader might need a pause for breath.

As with the previous books, it was decided from the outset only to use titles and honours coming before a contributor's name. This has the advantage of simplicity but it saddened me that, once again, some awards for bravery and honours of distinction have been left out. I apologize for that and I apologize, too, to some of the contributors whose choice could not be included either because of overlap or the strictures of copyright. The heroes' names have been left with every honour. Quotations by or about the heroes have been left without inverted commas. Comments by the contributors appear in quotation marks. The editorials are in smaller print and preceded by the symbol ¶.

The breadth of choice delighted me. I was touched by the accounts of family members who show heroism in a quiet way and hardly surprised that a mountaineer chose a former mountaineer or an oarsman, and a sailor chose the same all-time hero of the sea. One contributor commented, 'Our heroes reflect qualities that we sometimes aspire to'; yet a war photographer chose a conductor and an artist; and grand-daughter of an artist was not tempted by her famous grandfather, selecting instead a musician. The children have their own voice, and if we have a tiger in the sandpit or a granny who will save you if you fall off the fridge or the bunk-bed, who am I to gainsay them?

At the start of this venture I was unsure what we think a 'hero' to be. It seemed a rather outmoded concept. We are wary of hero-worship, preferring to talk of role models, and have no word for 'hero admiration'. The dictionary definition of a hero is plain enough: a man of courage, valour, ability, fortitude or greatness of soul; one admired for possessing exceptional qualities in connection with any pursuit, work or enterprise; the main protagonist in a poem, play or story. But compiling this book has given me, perhaps, a feel for more than that.

A friend sent me these words of Thucydides: 'The whole earth is the sepulchre of famous men. Their story is not graven only on stone over their clay, but abides everywhere, without visible symbol, woven into the fabric of other men's lives.'* The words of Florence

---

*From the oration over the fallen after the Battle of Marathon, *History of the Peloponnesian War*, Book 2, 43, iii.

Nightingale ring in my ears: 'I stand at the altar of the murdered men, and while I live I will fight their cause.' A holocaust survivor holds on to love at the very gates of hell. Another uses the last of his meagre ration of margarine to make a lamp on the eve of Chanukah and says, 'We once lived almost three days without water; but you cannot live properly for three minutes without hope.' Martyrs face their end with incredible fortitude. Hope, joy, love, tenacity, faith and the selfless act reverberate in my mind. Ronald Blythe, in his Foreword, tunes in to the words of the book; and if these words and the heroes they evoke enthral the reader as much as they have me, then I may be content.

GABRIELLA BAGLIETTO

Age 9, Lorretto Convent Junior School, Gibraltar

St Francis of Assisi

(1181–1226)

St Francis was a holy man,
He felt a sign that he must do all he can,
A church he was told to build,
Brick by brick, hand by hand
He worked and worked upon the sand.

St Francis loved the animals,
He loved the entire world.
He lived at one with nature,
And loved its creator.

Gabriella Baglietto

THE DUCHESS OF ABERCORN

Rainer Maria Rilke

(1875–1926)

Turning

Work of seeing is achieved,
now for some heart-work
on all those images, prisoned within you; for you
surmounted them, but do not yet know them.
Behold, O man within, the maiden within you! –
woman wrung from a thousand natures, woman
only outwrung, but never,
as yet, belov'd.

Rainer Maria Rilke

'I have found Rilke to be an inspiration over many years.'

¶ Rilke, probably the greatest German-language poet of the twentieth century, was born in Prague. He was a disciple of Rodin, with whom he worked for some years. He was influenced initially by French symbolism and wrote many poems in French. His advice to a young poet was, 'Go into yourself, search for the reason that bids you to write; find out whether you would have to die if it were denied you to write.'

BISHOP RIAH H. ABU EL-ASSAL
Thirteenth Anglican Bishop Emeritus in Jerusalem

Simon Sroji
(?–1939?)

May we meet soon in heaven.

Simon Sroji

'My great-uncle on my father's side, Simon Sroji, was a member of the Silesian Order and served its institutions in the surroundings of Jerusalem for many years. The people of Jerusalem and Nazareth testify to his very humble and holy life, but also to the fact that God empowered him to heal the sick by prayer and touching. The Church of Rome, after proper research and examinations, elevated him to that stage from where, by the grace of God, more evidence and testimonies will enable His Holiness the Pope to declare him as the second Palestinian saint in modern history. I still hold his last letter to my grandmother, written with his handwriting in 1939, in which he says that he thinks his days are numbered and begs her to be as ready as he is, so that when that day comes, both will be worthy to meet and see each other in heaven.'

~ ~

Violette Szabó GC

(1921–45)

The Life that I Have

The life that I have is all that I have
and the life that I have is yours.
And the love that I have of the life that I have
is yours and yours and yours.
A sleep I shall have, a rest I shall have,
yet death will be but a pause.
For the peace of my years in the long green grass
will be yours and yours and yours.

Attributed to Leo Marks (1920–2001),
code master for Violette Szabó

'Violette Szabó was certainly a heroine in her own right, but she also represents that group of incredibly brave men and women who fought in the Resistance in Europe during the war, facing very great danger, often torture and sometimes death, when they (like Violette) refused to betray their colleagues.'

❡ Violette Szabó was also chosen by her daughter TANIA SZABÓ, multilingual translator, who sent a tribute to her mother which included these lines:

You are the mother
I could not know.
Except by another
I could not grow.

Violette Bushell was the daughter of an English taxi driver and a French mother. She lived in Paris and then London. Leaving school, she worked as a hairdresser and then in Woolworth's. In 1940 she married Etienne Szabó, who was later killed at El Alamein. This loss inspired her to join the SOE (Special Operations Executive) helping the French resistance. She had one successful mission in France despite being arrested by the police. On her second mission she was captured while giving covering fire to a resistance fighter. She was tortured by the Gestapo and sent to Ravensbrück concentration camp where she was executed shortly before the liberation. She was awarded the George Cross and Croix de Guerre.

Leo Marks was code master for SOE during the Second World War, and the greatest code master of his time. Violette needed an unknown but easily remembered poem as a code, and Marks gave her these lines written by him in memory of the woman he loved. Violette adored the poem and asked him who had written it. He responded, 'I will tell you when you get back', though, in his heart, he knew the chances of her returning were remote.

The Violette Szabó Museum is to be found in the hamlet of Wormelow near Hereford. As a child, Violette, then in Lòndon, used to visit her aunt and her five lively cousins in this house.

OLINDA ADEANE

Journalist

Voltaire (Francois Marie Arouet)

(1694–1778)

Il faut cultiver notre jardin. (We must cultivate our garden.)

Voltaire, from *Candide*

'I was at a stuffy French school where discovering Voltaire was like opening a window onto fresh air. He is my hero because I like his name and he was surprising. He was brave when it was dangerous to say what you thought or to stick up for other people, but most of all I love his perfect and sparing words. Best of all, I find these words attributed to him helpful when my mind is unquiet: "Madness is to think of too many things in succession too fast or of one thing too exclusively".'

⁓ ⁓

HM King Hussein bin Talal

(1935–99)

All that we hope for is that a day will come, when we have all gone, when people will say that this man has tried, and his family tried. This is all there is to seek in the world.

HM King Hussein bin Talal

'These are words spoken by my father.'

Sir Mark Allen

Author and former diplomat

⁓ ⁓

St Teresa of Avila

(1515–82)

These interior matters are so obscure to the mind that anyone with as little learning as I will be sure to have to say many superfluous and irrelevant things in order to say a single one that is to the point . . . we continually hear what a good thing prayer is, and our Constitutions oblige us to engage in it for so many hours daily, yet they tell us nothing beyond what we ourselves have to do and say very little about the work done by the Lord in the soul – I mean supernatural work.

St Teresa of Avila, from *The Interior Castle*, I ii

'Teresa, the Carmelite saint and Doctor of the Church, wrote this when she was 62, five years before she died. Teresa was an enormous personality, intensely feminine, full of genius and human frailty, hardheaded, down to earth, yet warm and affective. Her writings give us her insights into the interior life – our own complexities and our blocks against the secret straightforwardness of God. Here, she underlines a vital truth we so easily forget: prayer is not what we do for God, but what he does in us, secretly.'

¶ St Teresa of Avila was also chosen by MICHAEL BARNETT, artist and sufferer from schizophrenia, who said, 'I often read St Teresa's *Road to Perfection* and *The Interior Castle* and I am struck by the way she had her own thoughts but was also assailed by thoughts, voices, visions and other-worldly experiences, some of which must have been terrifying and painful. It's almost as if she suffered from the same syndrome as me. And yet through faith and love of God and his love of her she transformed it into something sublime.'

PETER ALLISS

Professional golfer and television commentator

His Holiness the Dalai Lama

(1935–)

True friendship develops on the basis of human affection, not money or power. Of course, due to your power or wealth more people may approach you with big smiles or gifts. But deep down these are not real friends of yours, these are friends of your wealth or power. As long as your fortune remains, then these people often approach you, but when your fortunes decline they will no longer be there. With this type of friend nobody will make a sincere effort to help you if you need it. That is a reality . . . therefore the more you show concern about the welfare and rights of others, the more you are a genuine friend; the more you will remain open and sincere, then ultimately more benefits will come to you. If you forget or do not bother about others, then you will lose your own benefit.

From *The Dalai Lama's Little Book of Wisdom*

'I've never really considered myself a "religious" person, although I've tried to live a good life! Over the past few years I have been struck by the teachings of Buddha and the writings of the Dalai Lama on friendship and values.'

LORD ARMSTRONG OF ILMINSTER

Retired civil servant

Ralph Vaughan Williams

(1872–1958)

... Music imbued with greatness of soul.

> Wilfred Mellors, writing about the Fifth Symphony
> of Vaughan Williams in *Music and Society*

'Ralph Vaughan Williams, great of heart, noble of mind, and generous of spirit was, I believe, the greatest English composer of the twentieth century. I know that he is, quite simply, the greatest man I have known. He taught my father composition at the Royal College of Music, and they became lifelong friends. I first met him when I was an undergraduate at Oxford in 1947, and we became friends when he went back to live in London for the last five years of his life.'

THE VERY REVD DR JOHN ARNOLD

Dean Emeritus of Durham and former President of the
Conference of European Churches

Dietrich Bonhoeffer

(1906–45)

The difference between the Christian hope of resurrection and a mythological hope is that the Christian hope sends a man back to his life on earth in a wholly new way ... The Christian, unlike the devotees of the salvation myths, does not need a last refuge in the eternal from earthly tasks and difficulties. But like Christ himself ('My God, my God, why hast thou forsaken me?') he must drink the earthly cup to the lees, and only in his doing that is the crucified and risen Lord with him, and he (is) crucified and risen with Christ. This world must not be prematurely written off ... Christ takes hold of a man in the centre of his life.

> Dietrich Bonhoeffer, from *Letters and Papers from Prison*

'Bonhoeffer's words acquire added authority from his martyrdom on Sunday 8 April 1945 by Hitler's express command, a week before Flossenburg (the concentration camp where he was held) was liberated. There is here a curious parallel with St Luke's account of the crucifixion with the centurion's words, "Surely this was a righteous man" in that an SS doctor with the rank of captain (which is roughly equivalent to centurion) witnessed Bonhoeffer's execution and later wrote: "Through the half-open door . . . I saw Pastor Bonhoeffer . . . kneeling on the floor praying fervently to his God. I was most deeply moved by the way this lovable man prayed; so devout and so sure that God heard his prayer. At the place of execution he again said a short prayer and then climbed the steps to the gallows, brave and composed . . . In the almost 50 years I have worked as a doctor, I have hardly ever seen a man die so entirely submissive to the will of God".'

RT HON. LORD PADDY ASHDOWN
Politician

William Gladstone

(1809–98)

Oh William! If you were not such a great man you would be *very* boring.

Gladstone's wife, Catherine (1812–1900)

'Thus spoke Gladstone's wife, about the Grand Old Man.'

¶ Catherine Gladstone, a woman of exceptional charm, wit and discretion, was devoted to her husband. Two other women had refused him, but this marriage gave him a secure base of happiness until the end of his life. They had eight children.

Dame Eileen Atkins

Actress

꧁ ꧂

Virginia Woolf

(1882–1941)

Women have served all these centuries as looking-glasses possessing the magic and delicious power of reflecting the figure of man at twice its natural size.

Life for both sexes – and I looked at them, shouldering their way along the pavement – is arduous, difficult, a perpetual struggle. It calls for gigantic courage and strength. More than anything, perhaps, creatures of illusion as we are, it calls for confidence in oneself.

Without self-confidence we are as babes in the cradle.

Virginia Woolf, from her extended essay, *Room of One's Own*

'If confidence came in a bottle I'd make it obligatory for the National Health Service to give a spoonful to everyone once a week. Virginia Woolf may have been an atheist, but nevertheless I would call her writing inspirational and spiritual.'

Gillian Avery

Novelist and critic

꧁ ꧂

Cardinal John Henry Newman

(1801–90)

If I looked into a mirror and did not see my face, I should have the sort of feeling which actually comes upon me when I look into this living, busy world, and see no reflection of its creator.

J. H. Newman

¶ John Henry Newman was also chosen by the REVD PROFESSOR E. W. NICHOLSON, former Provost of Oriel College, Oxford. He quoted Newman's words about the man of the world who should, '. . . if he be an unbeliever, be too profound and large-minded to ridicule religion and too wise to be a dogmatist or fanatic' and noted that these were apt thoughts for today's 'secular fanatics'.

Professor Nicholson also told me this story on inter-faith dialogue. A rabbi and a priest were discussing a particularly difficult passage from Isaiah and could not agree upon the correct interpretation. The rabbi said, 'When I get to heaven, that is the first question I shall ask Isaiah about.' The priest asked, 'What if Isaiah isn't in heaven?' and was told, 'In that case you must ask him.'

SIR ALAN AYCKBOURN
Playwright/theatre director

Anton Chekhov
(1860–1904)

Brevity is the sister of talent.

Anton Chekhov, in a letter to Alexander Chekhov in 1889

'I admire Chekhov for his plays, for his brevity, seldom wasting a word, and for his accuracy of human observation. He's absolutely right. There is nothing *really* important that cannot be said in a few words or drawn with a few lines – certainly nothing that cannot fit on the single side of a postcard.'

ROBIN BAIRD-SMITH
Publisher

St John of the Cross
(1542–91)

God is the darkness in our light. Live in faith and hope though it be in darkness, for in the darkness God protects the soul.

St John of the Cross

'St John of the Cross, Spanish mystic, Carmelite friar and priest, was born in Fontiveros, a small village near Avila. Along with St Teresa of Avila he was founder of the Discalced Carmelites. He is also known for his writings. His poetry and studies on the growth of the soul are considered the summit of Spanish mystical literature and one of the peaks of all Spanish literature. He was canonized in 1762 and is one of the 33 doctors of the Church.

At ten to five on the evening of Saturday 8 January 1994, a young man in a white Volvo drove into me at 70 mph. My wife was killed instantly. One of my three children lived for two days and then died of his injuries. I was quite badly injured. Why did St John of the Cross become one of my heroes?

In my own inner turmoil, confusion and anger at what had happened to me, I knew that one thing that faith would never give me would be certainty. The phrase I most like about faith is "darkness". As we grow as human beings we need to dispense with props. God is not a funk hole or an oxygen tank. Even spiritual advisers can be obstacles. Ultimately we have to pursue the truth. "If it ever", wrote Simone Weil, "comes to a choice between Jesus and the Truth, we must always chose Truth. Disloyalty to Truth will always prove in the long run to have been disloyalty to Jesus."

In my feeble attempts at this, St John of the Cross has been my hero and my guide.'

JACK BECKEY

Age 9, Ash School, Somerset

My Mum

Doing all the washing up every day,
cooking meals and delicious food.
Caring for her family,
cleaning up after me
and loving us and wiping our tears.

Jack Beckey

G. K. Chesterton

(1874–1936)

I don't believe in the fate that falls on a man however they act, but I do believe in the fate that falls on them unless they act.

G. K. Chesterton

'Chesterton was brilliant at expressing profound truths in a very simple, memorable and at times paradoxical way. One of my favourites is that 'If a thing is worth doing, it is worth doing badly.' In the sentiment above, Chesterton is not attacking someone's inertia or laziness, but their lack of conviction and commitment. To sit idly by is a denial and a waste in the great adventure of life.'

Dame Joan Bakewell

Writer and broadcaster

Elizabeth Fry

(1780–1845)

Punishment is not for revenge, but to lessen crime and reform the criminal.

Elizabeth Fry, from her journal,
quoted in the *Biography of Distinguished Women* (1876)

'I have chosen this quotation from Elizabeth Fry because she pioneered a new way of dealing with criminal behaviour that is still needed today. I believe, as she did, that existing criminal provision is not helping reduce crime and needs a whole new approach. I admire her courage, generosity and foresight.'

¶ Born into a wealthy Quaker family in Norwich, Elizabeth had, even as a girl, great strength of purpose, clarity and independence of thought and kindness of heart. She married the London merchant Joseph Fry in 1800 and had many children. Despite these commitments she frequently visited Newgate, the local prison. The conditions, both physical and mental, were appalling. She started an association for female prisoners and obtained separation of the sexes, female guardians for women, access to employment, education and spiritual guidance and special treatment for violent criminals. Her influence spread through the United Kingdom and beyond. She travelled throughout Europe and wrote exhaustive reports to numerous governments. By the time of her death, many of her reforms, which also improved conditions in hospitals and mental asylums, had been put into action.

CLARE BALDING

Sports writer, commentator and champion rider

A. P. McCoy

(1974–)

He is a man apart.

J. P. McManus, the Irish racehorse owner, on A. P. McCoy

'There are many sportsmen and women whom I admire for their dedication, bravery and ability to perform under pressure, but I believe A. P. McCoy outstrips any other.

From the very first year he arrived from Ireland, he has been the leading rider in Britain and he once said, "I want to be champion until the day I retire."

McCoy genuinely cares about horses and people, and despite the effort that goes into riding at racecourses up and down the country, the danger that he faces every day and his painfully rigorous diet, he is always generous and willing to give a kind word to those who need it.'

¶ A. P. McCoy was also chosen by ALASDAIR MCWHIRTER, Creative Director, Ideas Network and son of Norris McWhirter, the co-founder of the *Guinness Book of Records*, with these words:

'Sportsmen often get more adulation than they deserve but "A.P." (McCoy) is an exception. Tiger Woods, Roger Federer and Michael Shumacher are all remarkable sportsmen but A. P. makes them look like amateurs.

Anthony Peter McCoy, born in Moneyglass, Co. Antrim, has ridden more than 2,750 "jump" winners and is now relentlessly homing in on his target of 3,000 victories: even Richard Dunwoody's previous record of 1,699 winners pales by comparison. Few jump jockeys ride for more than a month without breaking a bone and, in the course of his career, A.P. has broken almost every one of the 206 in his body (some more than a dozen times). At 5ft 10ins, he has had to starve himself for 18 years to keep to his racing weight.

In a sport where few remain at the top for long, the fracture of two of A.P.'s vertebrae did not interfere with him winning the title of Champion Jockey for the thirteenth season in a row. He thinks nothing of having a bad fall, knocking four teeth out, picking himself up and hurrying back to the paddock for his next ride – even though the horse has no realistic hope of winning.

Losing seems to be more painful to A.P. than physical discomfort, and yet he is always kind, gracious and, contrary to popular belief, witty.'

TOBY BALDING

Racing trainer

Lester Piggott

(1935–)

'I was lucky enough over 50 years to have been a trainer during a period of great horses, trainers and jockeys, and over this time the greatest influence for me was Lester Piggott. Though no saint, he rode, among many, for two of the truly great trainers, Noel Murless and Vincent O'Brien, both of whom would testify to his genius. Lester was a charismatic character and a legend in his own lifetime. Not only was he a fine jockey, he could judge his own mount and the others in a race with great speed and accuracy.

He once rode a horse called Moonlighter for my brother Ian at Newbury. It had been placed in several races and was a half-brother to Silly Season. We knew it was a stayer, so we planned with Lester that another horse would make the running, which it did, with Moonlighter happily following. At just the right moment Lester overtook and won the race with consummate ease. I had visions of the St Leger. But Lester, on dismounting, said, "He's no bloody good you know" and stumped off. He was right. The horse never won another race.

A taciturn man with a distinctive speech impediment, he gained a reputation for meanness which he rather played to. On one occasion he owed his head travelling lad the customary share-out following a win. Despite many reminders this was not forthcoming. Finally the lad cornered him and shouted in his ear, "Lester, you owe me and the boys five pounds." Lester parried, "I'm deaf in that ear." The lad went round to the other side and shouted more loudly, "Lester, you owe us a tenner." "You had better come round to the five-pound side" was the deadpan reply. The trouble was, you could forgive him anything, he was such a genius.'

The Rt Revd Michael Ball

The Rt Revd Edward King

(1829–1910)

It was a terrible privilege, but I am most thankful that I was allowed to be with the poor dear man. He was most beautiful; and his last (and first) Communion on Sunday morning put me to shame. I felt unworthy of him. How little the world knows of the inner life.

The Rt Revd Edward King, from *Search for a Saint: Edward King*
by John A. Newton

'Edward King, professor of moral theology at Oxford and then Bishop of Lincoln from 1885 to 1910, was arguably the holiest and most pastoral Anglican Bishop of the last 200 years. He was loved by all, from the highest to the lowliest; but not by the pompous. He visited a young murderer in Lincoln jail, whom he converted, confirmed, and to whom he gave the sacrament just before the lad was hanged – but King was condemned in *The Times* which expressed outrage that a prelate should consort with such a person. He is loved too for his profound and humble catholicity. Edward King is celebrated on 8 March in the Anglican Calendar of Saints.'

The Rt Revd George Bell

(1883–1958); Bishop of Chichester 1929–58

With Christ death is transcended.

> George Bell, from *The Church and Humanity*:
> the sermon 'And if Thine Enemy Hunger', broadcast 1946

'To introduce a stranger in a few words is difficult: but it is easy to see George Bell in his sixties and seventies; the Bishop of Chichester, with profuse white hair, shining blue eyes and a round face that radiated interest in you. He was "everything", and I believe he still is: as a saint of God, poet, biographer, pastor, husband, diplomat, almost a secret agent, and an old-fashioned bishop who knew his priests and people. In the Second World War, by extraordinary means he squeezed countless people from Hitler's Germany into the safety of Sweden. He was the great voice in the House of Lords against the dreadful bombing of Dresden, and probably because of this forfeited being Archbishop of Canterbury. He longed for the unity of Christ's Church, and together with Kathleen Bliss and others helped found the World Council of Churches.

Above all, he was holy. His eyes showed that he had seen God – and he added fun to this. An Irish priest not known for total honesty turned up late for a meeting. "Very sorry my lord," he said, "the bridge over the river at Newhaven was up." George Bell replied, "Impossible, low tide, sit down."

He will be celebrated as a saint in our strange Anglican way, at the altars of Chichester Cathedral on 3 October 2008, 50 years after his death.

Holy George, pray for us.'

GULALAI BAQI

Senior interpreter with the Medical Foundation for the
Treatment of Victims of Torture

Sa'di Shirazi

(1184–1291)

Learn how to be humble if you want to receive goodness,
Because the high land never receives water.

From *Gulistan* (*The Rose Garden*) by Sa'di Shirazi

'I have always enjoyed the poems of Sa'di Shirazi which are chiefly about love, and Sufism. They often have a message based on an old proverb whose words are woven into the verse.'

❡ Sa'di Shirazi's father died when he was a child, and he was educated in Shiraz, the 'city of poets', at the famous Islamic Nizamiya College. Following the Mongol invasion of Persia, he fled and travelled all over Africa, India and central Asia. In Syria he was captured by the Franks, and worked in the trenches of the fortress at Tripoli. Following his release he lived in Shiraz where, in his old age, he wrote his most famous prose and poetry. One of the messages given in the *Gulistan* is that 'a salutary lie is admitted to be preferable to a blunt truth.'

DR NICK BARNES

Paediatrician

W. C. Fields

(1880–1946); anti-hero

'W. C. Fields, American juggler, comic and actor, could hardly be described as a hero and was not known for his spirituality. It is reported that when he was gravely ill, a friend discovered him reading the Bible, asked him why, and his response was, "I'm looking for loopholes."

Fields assiduously played the part of anti-hero and misanthropist. Nonetheless, by behaving badly he illuminated the problem of how to behave well, better than many a worthy philanthropist. He was responsible for many pleasing insights, and is reputed to have said, "Horse sense is the thing a horse has which keeps it from betting on people".'

DAVID BARRIE

Director of the Art Fund

John Ruskin

(1819–1900)

There was no thought in any of us for a moment of their being clouds. They were clear as crystal, sharp on the pure horizon sky, and already tinged with rose by the sinking sun. Infinitely beyond all that we had ever thought or dreamed – the seen walls of lost Eden could not have been more beautiful to us: nor more awful, round heaven, the walls of sacred Death.

John Ruskin, on first sight of the Alps as a child

I am able, with yet happier and calmer heart than ever heretofore, to enforce its simplest assurance of Faith, that the knowledge of what is beautiful leads on, and is the first step, to the knowledge of the things which are lovely and of good report; and that the laws, the life, and the joy of beauty in the material world of God, are as eternal and sacred parts of his creation as, in the world of spirits, virtue; and in the world of angels, praise.

John Ruskin, from the epilogue to his five-volume
magnum opus, *Modern Painters*

'Leaving aside people I have actually known, I cannot think of anyone who has influenced me more than John Ruskin. I suppose he is best known today as a great writer and art critic. But for me, he is more than that. Artist, educator, social reformer, teacher, geologist, philanthropist – and the first person to suggest a charity to help museums and galleries acquire works of art.

Like Wordsworth, Ruskin was entranced by the wonders of the natural world – and mountains were always a source of inspiration for him.

The second quote sets out Ruskin's views on the relationship between art, spirituality and morality. These views are no longer fashionable but I still find his words very moving.'

PHIL BATES

A founder member of Samaritans in Dublin

Mother Teresa

(1910–97)

Look around you, at your family, your workmates, your neighbours. Loneliness is the disease of mankind. To be unloved and uncared for is poverty of the soul, and we must each try to ease that loneliness wherever we live.

It is not how much we do, but how much love we put in the doing. It is not how much we give, but how much love we put in the giving.

Mother Teresa

'I had the honour and pleasure of meeting Mother Teresa during her visit to Dublin in the 1970s. She spoke to us about her work in India. At the end of her talk several people, mostly women, jumped up offering to go and share in that work. She paused for a while, and speaking slowly and almost sternly, gave us these messages.'

RABBI DR TONY BAYFIELD

Rabbi Hugo Gryn

(1930–96)

It was the cold winter of 1944 and although we had nothing like calendars, my father who was my fellow-prisoner there [in the concentration camp], took me and some of our friends to a corner in our barrack. He announced that it was the eve of Chanukah, produced a curious-shaped clay bowl, and began to light a wick immersed in his precious, now melted, margarine ration. Before he could recite the blessing, I protested at this waste of food. He looked at me – then at the lamp – and finally said: 'You and I have seen that it is possible to live up to three weeks without food. We once lived almost three days without water; but you cannot live properly for three minutes without hope!'

Rabbi Hugo Gryn

'Hugo Gryn was 14 years old when that incident took place. He survived the Shoah (Holocaust) though his father and the rest of his family did not. After many adventures, Hugo became the rabbi of one of London's most important synagogues.

He is my hero (as he was my teacher and friend) because, despite experiences of unspeakable brutality and degradation, he never lost his faith in human beings. He went on to devote the whole of his life to building bridges between people and bringing out the best in human beings. Whenever someone spoke to Hugo, he made that person feel as though they were the most important person in Hugo's life. From the depths of dehumanization, he rose to the heights of confirmation that every human being is unique and infinitely precious.'

The Prophet Micah

(735–665 BC)

In the last days
the mountain of God's house shall be set firm
on the top of the mountains,
and raised up above the hills.

Then they will hammer their swords into ploughshares
and their spears into pruning-hooks.
nation shall not lift up sword against nation,
never again shall they train for war.
but everyone will sit under their vine and under their fig tree
and no one will terrorise them.

Micah 4.1, 3–4

'It is staggering to think that those words were spoken by the prophet Micah more than 2,700 years ago, also because many of the phrases have become part of the wealth of the English language and have been adopted by institutions far removed from Israel of long ago; also because of the extent to which that prophetic vision has become part of the vision, the dream of so many people around the world. When I hear the phrase "the legacy of Judaism", this is the kind of aspiration I think of.

Above all, it is staggering because it is so immediate and relevant today. "Everyone (Jew and Gentile alike) will sit under their vine and under their fig tree, *and no one will terrorise them*".'

THE RT HON. TONY BENN

Politician

Three men of Peace

Truth and reconciliation must be the basis for peace.

Archbishop Desmond Tutu (1931–)

'The three greatest moral leaders in my lifetime were Mahatma Gandhi, who championed non-violence in place of bloodshed; Nelson Mandela, who was sentenced to life imprisonment and then won the Nobel Peace Prize and became President of South Africa; and Archbishop Desmond Tutu, who developed the idea of truth and reconciliation as the basis of peace and progress. I have had the privilege of meeting all three of them, and I believe that they still offer the best way forward for humanity.'

TIMOTHY BENTINCK

Actor (David Archer in BBC Radio 4's *The Archers*)

Douglas Adams

(1952–2001)

Mathematical analysis and computer modelling are revealing to us that the shapes and processes we encounter in nature – the way that plants grow, the way that mountains erode or rivers flow, the way that snowflakes or islands achieve their shapes, the way that light plays on a surface, the way milk folds and spins into your coffee as you stir it, the way laughter sweeps through a crowd of people – all these things in their seemingly magical complexity can be described by the interaction of mathematical processes that are, if anything, even more magical in their simplicity . . .

. . . I think that the closest that human beings come to expressing our understanding of these natural complexities is in music. It is the most abstract of the arts – it has no meaning or purpose other than to be itself. Every single aspect of a piece of music can be represented by numbers. From the organisation of movements in a whole symphony, down through . . . all the elements of a noise that distinguish between the sound of one person piping on a piccolo and another one thumping a drum, can be expressed by patterns and hierarchies of numbers.

Some people object to such a view of music, saying that if you reduce music to mathematics, where does the emotion come into it? I would say that it's never been out of it. The things by which our emotions can be moved – the shape of a flower or a Grecian urn . . . the way daffodils flutter in the breeze, the way in which the person you love moves their head, the way their hair follows that movement, the curve described by the dying fall of the last chord of a piece of music – all these things can be described by the complex flow of numbers. That's not a reduction of it, that's the beauty of it.

Douglas Adams, from *Dirk Gently's Holistic Detective Agency*

'I first came across Douglas Adams through *The Hitchhiker's Guide to the Galaxy*, and I was struck by his intelligence, imagination and humour. My father was an environmentalist and a philosopher (and had introduced me to James Lovelock, author of the *Gaia* books) and after his death I identified very much with Adams, who had the same type of enquiry and fascination with the world and why we are here. He was bright and funny and, like myself, very tall and "nerdy", as early computer buffs seemed to be. The passage above is one of my favourites and asks the impossible question, "Is God a mathematician?".'

ANIL BHANOT

General Secretary of the Hindu Council in the UK

✎ ✎

Rabindranath Tagore

(1861–1941)

Lost Star

When the creation was new and all the stars shone in their first
splendour, the gods held their assembly in the sky and sang
'Oh, the picture of perfection! The joy unalloyed!'

But one cried, all of a sudden
'It seems that somewhere there is a break in the chain of light
and one of the stars has been lost.'

The golden string of their harp snapped,
their song stopped, and they cried in dismay
'Yes, that star was the best,
she was the glory of all heavens!'

From that day the search is unceasing for her,
and the cry goes on from one to the other
that in her the world has lost its one joy!

Only in the deepest silence of the night the stars smile
and whisper among themselves
'Vain is this seeking! Unbroken perfection is over each and all!'

Rabindranath Tagore, No. 7 from *Gitanjali*

'Rabindranath Tagore won the Nobel Prize for Literature in 1913, a
poet whose literary works, music and paintings were always inter-
woven with a mystical message. In the poem "Lost Star" Tagore's
message is to appreciate God's Creation for what it is in the here and
now rather than to lament the past or cling to an imaginary hope of
one's own making; for the hope to see God's beauty only in one
uniform whole is to miss the very point of his diverse Creation, the
same one truth through many paths.'

MARY BIGGART

Grandmother

Isaac of Nineveh

(Seventh-century Kurdish Desert Father)

The tree of life is the love of God from which Adam fell away. Thereafter he met with joy no longer, but toiled and wearied himself in the land of thorns.

Until we find love, our labour is in that land of thorns; amidst thorns we both sow and reap, even if our seed is the seed of righteousness.

But once we have found love, we partake of the heavenly bread, being nourished without labour and fatigue.

Whoever is sustained on love is sustained by Christ who is God over all.

Love is the kingdom in which the Lord mystically promised that his disciples should eat and drink.

Isaac of Nineveh, taken from
Heart of Compassion – Daily Readings with St Isaac of Syria

'When I found this little book, my heart was immediately lifted by Isaac's wise words about God's love for all of us, the wide open door of God's compassion, and his teaching about prayer and the gift of tears.'

❡ Isaac of Nineveh (also known as Isaac of Syria) was also chosen by the REVD LADY DURAND.

COLONEL JOHN BLASHFORD-SNELL

Explorer and scientist

Brigadier Peter Young, DSO, MC and Two Bars

(1915–88)

Dear boys, you look like the sort of evil pair who might like a bit of . . . loot and pillage.

Brigadier Peter Young

'This is how Peter Young addressed me and John (now Professor) Adair, when he asked us to represent the Commonwealth side in a re-enactment of the Civil War.

Peter, under whom I served as an instructor at Sandhurst, was one of the most charismatic, courageous and brilliant officers I ever met. An acknowledged expert on military history, he was great fun to work with and had those essential qualities of leadership – being able to communicate and inspire – and, in a quiet way, was a sincere God-fearing man.

He had commanded the 9th Arab Regiment under Glub Pasha and, holding no fewer than three Military Crosses and the DSO, was indeed a legend.'

¶ Peter Young was the founder of the Civil War re-enactment society, The Sealed Knot, and was its 'Captain Generall' [*sic.*].

ERIN WARD

Age 11, Omagh Integrated School, Co. Tyrone

Robin Hood

Arrow Shooter,
Strange Dresser,
Trouble Maker,
Great Fighter.

Lucretius

99–55 BC

Tantum religio potuit suadere malorum.
(So much evil could religion prompt.)

Titus Lucretius Carus

'Why is he a hero? I think because he puts the case for a humane rationalism, and against religious or ideological intolerance, so passion-
ately. The world about us, whether it be the stars or the animals in
the fields, is to him the real miracle. In many ways he is the first
Enlightenment Man. He would have loathed religious extremists but
would have advocated arguing with them rather than shooting them.
We need more like him today.'

❡ Lucretius is also quoted as saying: *Inque brevi spatio mutantur saecla animan-
tum et quasi cursores vitai lampada tradunt* (The generations of living things
pass in a short time and, like runners, hand on the torch of life).

RONALD BLYTHE

Writer

Thomas Traherne

(1637?–74)

The corn was orient and immortal wheat, which never should be reaped, nor was ever sown. I thought it had stood from everlasting to everlasting. The dust and stones of the street were as precious as gold. The gates were at first the end of the world, the green trees when I saw them first through one of the gates transported and ravished me; their sweetness and unusual beauty made my heart to leap, and almost mad with ecstasy, they were such strange and wonderful things: the men! O what venerable and reverend creatures did the aged seem! Immortal cherubims! And young men glittering and sparkling angels and maids strange seraphic pieces of life and beauty! Boys and girls tumbling in the street, and playing, were moving jewels. I knew not that they were born or should die. But all things abided eternally as they were in their proper places. Eternity was manifest in the light of the day . . . the city seemed to stand in Eden, or to be built in Heaven . . . and all the world was mine, and I the only spectator and enjoyer of it.

Thomas Traherne, from *Centuries of Meditations*

'This is the poet-priest Thomas Traherne recalling his boyhood in Hereford, *c.* 1650. He is an ecstatic writer who so loved being alive that he believed that every moment should be visionary and packed with gratitude for what God had given him. I "met" Traherne in my youth and he has long been my hero.'

SANDRA BOLER

Journalist and former editor of *Brides* magazine

St Peter

(First century)

Thou art Peter, and upon this rock I will build my church.

Matthew 16.18 (AV)

'Christ's choice of St Peter above all others, to be the bedrock of the Church, reassures me that Christ understood the frailty and weakness of mankind. In this most human of saints who betrayed Christ three times, we find this overwhelming example of divine faith in us. St Peter is a saint with whom we can all identify. The earliest known reference is found in Origen's Commentary (AD 186–253), which is older than any extant Greek manuscript. He says: "If we also say the same as Peter, 'Thou art the Christ, the Son of the living God', not by the instruction of flesh and blood, but by the illumination of the heavenly Father in our hearts, we ourselves become the same thing as Peter".'

ROSEMARY BOOTH

Retired teacher

Julian of Norwich

(*c.* 1342–post-1416)

When the soul is tempest tossed, troubled and cut off by worries, then is the time to pray . . . And so I saw that, whenever we feel the need to pray, our good Lord follows us, helping our desire . . . For I saw too, that his unceasing work in everything is done so well, so wisely and so mightily that it is beyond our power to imagine, or guess or think.

Julian of Norwich, from The Revelations of Divine Love

'The chaplain at the Julian cell who is a man of prayer, offered prayers for my daughter who underwent a spinal operation. Later my daughter and I stayed at the cell and since then I've recommended a visit there to friends in trouble.'

¶ Julian of Norwich was also chosen by PROFESSOR BENJAMIN LAMBERTON, Attorney and Professorial Lecturer in Law, who sent:

. . . Jesus Christ who does good for evil is our true mother; we have our being from him where the ground of motherhood begins, with all the sweet protections of love which follows eternally.

'I find Julian completely fascinating. Her generous consciousness and spiritual boldness give new life to traditional doctrines, none more so than the Trinity. She sees in Jesus an energy that transcends his physical gender. And she invites us to see the feminine as essential to his ministry. That's very liberating!'

THE RT HON. BARONESS BOOTHROYD

Former Speaker of the House of Commons

John F. Kennedy

(1917–63)

And so, my fellow Americans; ask not what your country can do for you – ask what you can do for your country. My fellow citizens of the world: ask not what America will do for you, but what together we can do for the freedom of man.

From John F. Kennedy's inaugural address on 20 January 1961

'I very much admired John Kennedy. I was there when he made his inauguration speech and believe that this passage from it is one of the most inspiring I have ever heard.'

COMMANDER N. S. BOWER

Submarine Commanding Officer

~~❦~~

Captain Noel Godfrey Chavasse, VC and Bar, MC, RAMC

(1884–1917)

Greater love hath no man than this, that a man lay down his life for his friends.

John 15.13: epitaph chosen for the grave of Captain Chavasse by his father, Francis James Chavasse, 2nd Bishop of Liverpool

During an attack he tended the wounded in the open all day, under heavy fire, frequently in view of the enemy. During the ensuing night he searched for wounded on the ground in front of the enemy's lines for four hours. Next day he took one stretcher-bearer to the advanced trenches, and, under heavy fire, carried an urgent case for 500 yards into safety, being wounded in the side by a shell splinter during the journey. The same night he took up a party of trusty volunteers, rescued three wounded men from a shell hole twenty-five yards from the enemy's trench, buried the bodies of two officers and collected many identity discs, although fired on by bombs and machine guns. Altogether he saved the lives of some twenty badly wounded men, besides the ordinary cases which passed through his hands. His courage and self-sacrifice were beyond praise.

The *London Gazette* citation for his first VC at Guillemot as the Medical Officer attached to 10th (Liverpool Scottish) Battalion, the King's (Liverpool) Regiment, in August 1916

Though severely wounded (bleeding profusely from his abdomen) early in the action whilst carrying a wounded soldier to the dressing station, he refused to leave his post, and for two days not only continued to perform his duties, but in addition, went out repeatedly under heavy fire to search for and attend to the wounded . . . Worn with fatigue and faint from his wound, . . . he was instrumental in rescuing many who would otherwise have succumbed. This devoted and gallant officer subsequently died of his wounds.

Derived from the *London Gazette*, 14 September 1917. Citation for the posthumous VC awarded for gallantry at Passchendaele from 31 July to 2 August 1917

'I was first made aware of Noel Chavasse as he was an ex-pupil of Magdalene College School where I was educated almost a century later. Receiving a Victoria Cross and Bar is an achievement in itself; however, the non-aggressive manner of his actions, beyond any concern for himself, is what I particularly admired. He remained determined to help others and this eventually cost him his life.'

MIKE BREARLEY

Former Captain of the England cricket team

Wilfred Bion

(1897–1979)

The object is to introduce the patient to the most important person he is ever likely to have dealings with, namely himself. It sounds simple; in fact it is extremely difficult. One is always liable to affect the patient with one's own views . . . The main object is to help the patient to be less frightened of his own horrible self – however horrible he thinks he is.

Wilfred Bion, from *Four Discussions with W. R. Bion*

'My hero is Wilfred Bion, psychoanalyst, who radically shifted psychoanalytic ideas between the 1950s and his death in the late 1970s.'

ARMAN HAIDER

Age 12, Lorretto Convent Junior School, Gibraltar

Donald Bradman

(1908–2001)

Of course he was sublime,
The greatest batsman of all time,
Don Bradman with a swing of his bat
He could hit the ball with a mighty WHACK!

When he was fielding, his catch was soft as sand,
Right in the palm, that's where it would land.
He could also stop the ball from passing the rope,
He could run anyone out, no batsman had hope.

But on his last match that he would play,
To average one hundred he needed just three,
If he was bowled with no runs, he would have been shaken,
Just guess what happened – his wicket was taken!

But his legacy would never halt,
As everyone agreed, he never had any fault.
Now children everywhere want to get up and bat,
He was the greatest, we can say that!

Arman Haider

RICHARD BRIERS

Actor

Sir Henry Irving

(1838–1905)

First lay your lines. Settle what you have to do and do it. The greater
the opposition, the more persevering and courageous you must be.
If you are right, and strength and life hold out, you must win.

Sir Henry Irving

'Sir Henry Irving became the first Knight of the theatre in 1895 and, against all odds, ruled Victorian theatre for 15 years at the Lyceum. His love, and drive to succeed, is an inspiration to any young actor.'

RAYMOND BRIGGS

Author and illustrator (including *The Snowman*)

Wilfred Owen

(1893–1918)

This book is not about heroes. English poetry is not yet fit
　to speak of them.
Nor is it about deeds, or lands, nor anything about glory,
honour, might, majesty, dominion, or power, except War.
Above all I am not concerned with Poetry.
My subject is War, and the pity of War.
The Poetry is in the pity.

Wilfred Owen

'Wilfred Owen is someone I greatly admire, and the quotation I have chosen is from a famous preface that was found in an unfinished condition among his papers.'

Futility

Move him into the sun –
Gently its touch awoke him once,
At home, whispering of fields unsown.

Always it woke him, even in France,
Until this morning and this snow.
If anything might rouse him now
The kind old sun will know.

Think how it wakes the seeds, –
Woke, once, the clays of a cold star.
Are limbs, so dear-achieved, are sides,
Full-nerved – still warm – too hard to stir?
Was it for this the clay grew tall?
– O what made fatuous sunbeams toil
To break earth's sleep at all?

¶ Wilfred Owen, the son of a stationmaster, was born in Shropshire. Before the war he worked in a poor country parish, then taught in France. He enlisted in 1915 but, following concussion and trench fever, was invalided out to an Edinburgh hospital where he met and was encouraged by Siegfried Sassoon. He returned to France and won the MC but was killed on the Sambre Canal a week before the Armistice. His poems, some of the most poignant of the war, were mostly written between 1917 and 1918 and were published posthumously by Sassoon.

SARAH BROWN

Prime Minister's wife

Graça Machel (Mrs Nelson Mandela)

(1945–)

Children are the nucleus of sustainable human development. Relatively small investments in their health, education and welfare pay huge dividends for society.

Graça Machel

'From teacher to Education Minister to First Lady of Mozambique, Graça Machel has championed the rights and responsibilities for children all her life. Now on an international stage with her husband Nelson Mandela, Graça Machel is unflinching, unyielding and unhesitating in her quest to persuade countries to help alleviate child poverty and abuse in the world.

She is a phenomenally gracious woman who with determination takes on a tough role. That she also brings happiness to Nelson Mandela only serves to mark her out further. As Nelson Mandela touchingly said of Graça, "She is my life!".'

¶ Graça Machel married Nelson Mandela in 1998, her former husband Samora Machel, the President of Mozambique, having died in 1986.

CRAIG BROWN

Columnist and satirical writer

Henry James Sr

(1811–82)

Every man who has reached even his intellectual teens begins to suspect that life is no farce; that it is not genteel comedy even; that it flowers and fructifies on the contrary out of the profoundest tragic depths of the essential dearth in which its subject's roots are plunged. The natural inheritance of everyone who is capable of spiritual life is an unsubdued forest where the wolf howls and the obscene bird of night chatters.

Henry James Sr, writing to his sons Henry and William

'I have chosen this not only because it is such a wonderfully dramatic piece of writing, but because it is from an unsung hero – Henry James Sr – to his more celebrated sons, Henry the novelist, and William the philosopher and psychologist. Small wonder that the brothers became such giants in their fields when this was the type of letter their father sent them! My own children are now in their late teens, but I rarely sent them more than a postcard or two, probably amounting to a couple of dozen words of silly jokes and banalities. Henry James Sr was the kind of father who makes the rest of us feel pitiful.'

MICHAEL BROWN

Purveyor of smoked eels

Hilaire Belloc

(1870–1953)

From quiet homes and first beginnings,
Out to the undiscovered ends,
There's nothing worth the wear of winning
But laughter and the love of friends.

From The Complete Verse of Hilaire Belloc

'This was my father's favourite – his talisman – and with which he concluded his speech at his Golden Wedding Anniversary.'

DR RICHARD BUDGETT

CMO to the London Organizing Committee of the Olympic Games, 2012

Baron Pierre de Coubertin

(1863–1937)

The most important thing in the Olympic Games is not winning but taking part . . . The essential thing in life is not conquering but fighting well.

Baron Pierre de Coubertin, from a speech at a banquet for
officials of the Olympic Games, London, 24 July 1908

¶ Baron Pierre de Coubertin devoted his fortune and his life to the cause of reviving the International Olympic Games and was the leading figure in their revival in 1896 after nearly 1,500 years in abeyance. Though of French aristocratic birth he was a republican and became a progressive educationalist. He was influenced by the Shropshire doctor William Penny Brookes who, from 1850, had organized annual British Olympic Games in Much Wenlock, and the record of Robert Dover who, in 1612, had revived some yearly 'Olympick Games'.

The Rt Revd Thomas M. Burns
Roman Catholic Bishop to the Forces

Sir Humphrey Appleby

It is characteristic of all committee discussions and decisions that every member has a vivid recollection of them, and that every member's recollection of them differs violently from every other member's recollection; consequently we accept the convention that the official decisions are those and only those which have been officially recorded in the minutes by the officials; from which it emerges with elegant inevitability, that any decision which has been officially reached would have been officially recorded in the minutes by the officials, and any decision which is not recorded in the minutes by the officials has not been officially reached, even if one or more members believe they can recollect it; so in this particular case, if the decision would have been officially reached, it would have been recorded in the minutes by the officials, and it isn't so it wasn't.

Sir Humphrey Appleby, in *Yes Minister* by Sir Antony Jay

ED BUTLER

Brigadier Commander British Forces, Afghanistan, 2006

Theodore Roosevelt

(1858–1919)

It is not the critic who counts: not the man who points out how the strong man stumbles or where the doer of deeds could have done better. The credit belongs to the man who is actually in the arena, whose face is marred by dust and sweat and blood, who strives valiantly, who errs and comes up short again and again, because there is no effort without error or shortcoming, but who knows the great enthusiasms, the great devotions, who spends himself for a worthy cause; who, at the best, knows, in the end, the triumph of high achievement, and who, at the worst, if he fails, at least he fails while daring greatly, so that his place shall never be with those cold and timid souls who knew neither victory nor defeat.

Theodore Roosevelt, from the speech 'Citizenship in a Republic'
at the Sorbonne, Paris, 23 April 1910

'I am afraid that Roosevelt is neither a saint nor a particular hero of mine, but I do find his words very apt for some of the ventures I have undertaken and for today's generation of young men and women in the Armed Forces who have demonstrated courage "over and above", in Iraq, Afghanistan and many other operational theatres. They have certainly dared all and risked all. I was truly humbled by the consistent and utmost courage, fighting spirit and endurance shown by the 16 Air Assault Brigade Task Force in Afghanistan last year. Tragically, a good number were badly injured and many did not return.'

David

(?–*c.* 962 BC)

The heavens declare the glory of God; and the firmament sheweth his handywork.

Psalm 19.1 (AV)

'David was one of the greatest figures in the Old Testament, a courageous warrior, a successful general; a leader who united the tribes of Israel, and a poet. Many of his psalms described the wonders and the glory of the Lord. He was also human and behaved badly yet repented of his behaviour.

He felt abandoned by God: "My God, my God, why hast thou forsaken me? . . . I cry in the daytime, but thou hearest not; and in the night season, and am not silent . . . But I am a worm, and no man; a reproach of men, and despised of the people" (Psalm 22.1–2, 6). But he also wrote, "The LORD is my strength and my shield; my heart trusted in him, and I am helped: therefore my heart greatly rejoiceth; and with my song will I praise him" (Psalm 28.7).

His recognition of human frailty together with his complete trust in God and in God's forgiveness described in beautiful poetry makes David an inspiration to others, as he is to me.'

Dr Lavinia Byrne

Writer and Wells City Councillor

St Simeon Stylites

(c. 390–459)

'Here is a man for whom actions were more important than words – and on a grand scale. His story can be simply told: he was born at Sisan in northern Syria, the son of a shepherd. Syria became part of the Byzantine Empire in 395 and Christianity spread. Simon was converted and joined a monastery, but his excessive penances alarmed the other monks and the abbot wanted him to leave. He found an interesting outlet for his penitential spirit, deciding to live on a pillar. Food and drink were hauled up to him in a bucket on one pulley, and – one hopes – another bucket was used to bring down waste products. Now until I went to Syria and saw the remains of his pillar in the ruins of the basilica that was later built around it, I thought he was mad. More than that, I thought he was some kind of obsessive, with a fantasy about phalluses and seeing his own grow as he chose to build his pillar higher and higher. Eventually it was some 65 feet tall.

But then I saw the column in context, the slow, sweeping landscape that surrounds it, and I was entranced. Simon wanted to be close to God, literally, and stayed there for 37 years.

Saints are often sad, mad and bad. Their heroism was all about letting God come to them as they were, rather than pretending to be otherwise. So there is hope – and inspiration – for us all.'

Professor Sir Kenneth C. Calman

Chancellor, University of Glasgow and former Chief Medical Officer

John Hunter

(1728–93)

But why think? Why not trie the expt?'

John Hunter to Edward Jenner following a discussion on hedgehogs

'John Hunter is one of my real heroes. Born near Glasgow, in 1748 he joined his brother William, a distinguished physician and obstetrician, in London to learn medicine and in particular anatomy and surgery. John was the first real experimental surgeon, with a huge interest in animals and humans, and he maintained a zoo at his house in Earl's Court. He changed the face of surgery.

Always discovering fresh things, he once said to a student, "Never ask me what I have said or what I have written, but if you ask me what my present position is I will tell you." When asked about his views changing, he replied, "Very likely I did. I hope I grow wiser every year." A hard worker, he never seemed to sleep. He worked by experiment and careful recording of the findings. Full of curiosity, he was not afraid to try something new. What a hero!'

¶ Edward Jenner introduced the practice of vaccination for smallpox in 1796, in his practice in Berkeley, Gloucestershire.

SIR ROY CALNE
Transplant surgeon (first liver transplant)

Watson, Crick and the team discovering the structure of DNA

It has not escaped our notice that the specific pairing we have postulated immediately suggested a possible copying mechanism for the genetic material.

J. D. Watson and F. H. C. Crick, molecular structure of nucleic acids, from a paper in *Nature*, 25 April 1953

'Crick and Watson, with considerable help from the work of Rosalind Franklin and Maurice Wilkins, by discovering the structure of DNA provided a focal joining point for the evolutionary theories of Charles Darwin and the mathematical laws of inheritance described by Gregor Mendel. The short paper in *Nature* was the beginning of an evolution in biology, with ramifications in all branches of life science and particularly in medicine.

The creative personality of the two individuals has often been described. They talked and argued incessantly, made molecular models and enjoyed themselves in Cambridge in the 1950s.

The illustration of the double helix in *Nature* was drawn by Francis Crick's wife Odell, an accomplished artist, joining art to science.

I suppose that Crick and Watson were not quite heroes and certainly not saints, but they did unravel an important mystery which led to an extraordinary understanding of biology.'

W. B. Yeats

(1865–1939)

The Lover Tells of the Rose in his Heart

All things uncomely and broken, all things worn out and old,
The cry of a child by the roadway, the creak of a lumbering
     cart,
The heavy steps of the ploughman, splashing the wintry
     mould,
Are wronging your image that blossoms a rose in the deeps of
     my heart.
The wrong of unshapely things is a wrong too great to be told;
I hunger to build them anew and sit on a green knoll apart,
With the earth and the sky and the water, remade, like a casket
     of gold
For my dreams of your image that blossoms a rose in the
     deeps of my heart.

W. B. Yeats

'I particularly love this poem of Yeats, because of the first verse. That
"... cry of the child by the roadside ..." haunts me. Was it from tired-
ness, cold, ill-treatment or, in Yeats' day, more likely hunger? And
even if the Celtic tiger and the welfare state have changed the
prospects of many children in this special island, there are still too
many cries unanswered.'

TIMOTHY AND ELIZABETH CAPON

Retired company director and art gallery guide

Leonard Cheshire

(1917–92)

I am conscious that it is above everything else with people that I
have to do, with individual human beings, each a person in his own
right, unique and unrepeatable, each a member of our human
family destined for the same eternal end, with all the dignity and
responsibility that this implies.

Leonard Cheshire, from *Hidden World*

'Maybe it's our age, but I seem to find few "great" men or women who
do not have feet of clay. One exception, and the only person I have
ever met who seemed to combine greatness with obvious goodness,
was Leonard Cheshire. He seemed to have an aura of saintliness
about him which shone out like light.'

❡ In August 1945, Leonard Cheshire, an RAF bomber pilot, was an observer at
the dropping of the atom bomb on Hiroshima. Subsequently, he founded the
Cheshire Home Charity, which cares for physically and mentally disabled
people around the world. Becoming himself a victim of motor neurone disease,
he said to a friend, 'Now I really know how it feels to be in a wheelchair.' On
peace, Cheshire wrote in *Hidden World*: 'It is imperative that we recognise that
peace through justice is the concern of us all. The concern of each individual
person, each community, each political group, each nation.'

REAR ADMIRAL JAMES CARINE

Chairman of the Royal United Hospital, Bath

Aeneas Lee

Among the many large white marble plaques on the Minster walls in Ilminster extolling the deeds and virtues of the great and the good is a small brass plate which simply says:

> In memory of
> Aeneas Lee, AB
> who perished in Submarine 'B2' off Dover
> 4th Oct. 1912
> Aged 20
> A good son – a brave lad

'Clearly a hero in the eyes of his family, and what better epitaph could any man want?'

CARLA CARLISLE

Writer and farmer

Rachel Carson

(1907–64)

If I had influence with the good fairy who is supposed to preside over the christening of all children, I should ask that her gift to each child in the world be a sense of wonder so indestructible that it would last throughout life.

Only within the moment of time represented by the present century has one species – man – acquired significant power to alter the nature of the world.

Rachel Carson, from *The Sense of Wonder* and *Silent Spring*

Man has lost the capacity to foresee and to forestall. He will end by destroying the earth.

Albert Schweitzer (1875–1965), quoted by Rachel Carson in the
dedication to him of her book Silent Spring

'My heroine is Rachel Carson, a shy, generous and courageous woman who combined a prodigious scientific curiosity with a God-given gift for writing that was poetic and powerful. Her books, beginning with *The Sea Around Us*, redefined the way humans look at their place in nature.

Rachel Carson's hero was Albert Schweitzer, hence her dedication. Most days I share Schweitzer's – and Carson's – pessimism, but if there is hope for the future of our planet, it is in part because of Rachel Carson who opened our eyes to the damage that humans were causing to their earthly home.'

Deborah Cassidi
Retired doctor

St Peter
(First century)

And Peter remembered the word of Jesus, which said unto him, Before the cock crow, thou shalt deny me thrice. And he went out, and wept bitterly.

Matthew 26.75

'For me, these are some of the most moving words in the New Testament. Only hours before, Peter promised total allegiance. "Though I should die with thee, yet will I not deny thee." His failure is total, his regret heartbreaking, but in the end his redemption will be complete.'

Robert Louis Stevenson

(1850–94)

Requiem

Under the wide and starry sky,
Dig the grave and let me lie.
Glad did I live and gladly die,
    And I laid me down with a will.

This be the verse you grave for me:
Here he lies where he longed to be;
Home is the sailor, home from sea,
    And the hunter home from the hill.

'This was one of the first poems I learned when at a very small prep. school run by two redoubtable Quaker ladies. They knew everything about what was important: climbing trees, hiding under the stairs and reading fairy stories or *Treasure Island* during air raids, ballet lessons (from an exquisite teacher balancing on a piano stool), daily prayers and fair punishments. When I lit a fire in the bedroom to see what would happen, the result was up at six every morning for a week to clean and lay the school fires. I loved them, RLS and this poem in equal measure.'

❡ R. L. Stevenson also wrote *Kidnapped, The Master of Ballintrae, The Strange Case of Dr Jekyll and Mr Hyde, Travels with a Donkey*, many poems and the beautiful 'Vailima Prayers'.

Admiral Sir Desmond Cassidi
Retired naval officer

St Thomas Aquinas
(1225–74)

Give us O Lord, a steadfast heart, which no unworthy thought can drag downwards; an unconquered heart, which no tribulation can wear out; an upright heart, which no unworthy purpose may tempt aside. Bestow upon us also, O Lord our God, understanding to know Thee, diligence to seek Thee, wisdom to find Thee, and a faithfulness that may finally embrace Thee: through Jesus Christ Our Lord.

St Thomas Aquinas

'I came across this prayer while seeking material for a remembrance service. This caused me to read a little about St Thomas Aquinas. His output was prodigious, varying from commentaries on Aristotle to a treatise on biblical writings. After his death he was initially criticized but later recognized as a great Christian philosopher and theologian.'

Jainy Ann Joeman
Age 11, Omagh Integrated School, Co. Tyrone

Kangaroo Jack

High jumper,
Cool actor,
Camera lover,
Weird rapper.

Clever thinker,
Wonderful dancer,
Great fighter,
Fast runner.

Jainy Ann Joeman

John Donne

(1571?–1631)

We attribute but one privilege to Man's body, above other moving creatures, that he is not as others, grovelling, but of an erect, of an upright form, naturally built, and disposed to the contemplation of Heaven. Indeed it is a thankful form, and recompenses that soul which gives it, with carrying that soul so many foot higher, towards Heaven. Other creatures look to the earth; and even that is no unfit object, no unfit contemplation for Man; for thither he must come; but because Man is not to stay there, as other creatures are, Man in his natural form, is carried to the contemplation of that place, which is his home, Heaven.

John Donne, from the *Devotions of John Donne*

'I was best man at the wedding of a dear friend in still unblitzed Llandaff Cathedral and the delectable pair gave me the works of John Donne, which till then I did not know; and ever since I have loved the volume, and revered Donne: a great Christian teacher, and a master of the English language, in the flowering age not long before the Civil War.'

❡ John Donne was also chosen by Julian Pettifer, writer and broadcaster, who chose this poem:

The Sun Rising

Busy old fool, unruly sun,
Why dost thou thus,
Through windows, and through curtains call on us?
Must to thy motions lovers' seasons run?
Saucy pedantic wretch, go chide
Late school-boys, and sour prentices,
Go tell court-huntsmen, that the King will ride,
Call country ants to harvest offices;
Love, all alike, no season knows, nor clime,
Nor hours, days, months, which are the rags of time.

THE RT REVD JOHN BRYSON CHANE
Episcopal Bishop of Washington, in the District of Columbia

꙼ꙮ ꙮ꙼

An Anonymous Hero

A vision without a task is a dream.
A task without a vision is drudgery.
And a vision and a task is the hope of the world.

Anonymous quote, reputedly transcribed from
the wall of an Anglican church in Sussex

¶ No record of any memorial or plaque bearing these words could be found in church records for Sussex.

THE RT REVD AND RT HON. RICHARD CHARTRES
Bishop of London

꙼ꙮ ꙮ꙼

St Bishoi

(?320–417)

'There is in the desert a community whose Patron Saint is Bishoi. He received a visitation that if he went walking in a certain part of the desert he would meet Jesus Christ. He set out with his young disciples, and along the way they met an old man who had fallen down with exhaustion and was unable to get back to the cave in which he lived. He asked the young men for help and they said that they would be glad to help in any other circumstances but they had received a vision that they would meet Jesus Christ that day and they did not dare to miss that opportunity, so they continued on their way.

St Bishoi himself, however, when he came to the man said, "Spiritual visions are all very well, but nothing is more important than active love of our neighbour." He picked up the old man and carried him on his shoulders to the cave, and it was then that he saw that he had really been carrying Jesus Christ himself, and he was the only one for whom the vision came true.'

ANTHONY COCKSHUT

University teacher

St Martin de Porres

(1579–1639)

He loved men because he saw them as God's children and his own brothers. He loved them indeed more than himself, and in his humility believed everyone to be better and holier than he was.

From the homily of Pope John XXIII for the
canonization of St Martin de Porres, 6 May 1962

❡ Martin de Porres was a Dominican lay brother in Lima, Peru. His father was a Spanish grandee and his mother of slave descent. Initially a lay helper, having previously been apprentice to a barber-surgeon, he used those skills to help others. He was soon made a lay brother and worked with the poor, the sick and plague victims irrespective of race, colour or his own vulnerability. He was known as the 'father of charity' but called himself 'mulatto dog'. He is often cited as a patron of race relations.

Pope Pius IX

(1792–1878)

For his comment to the Anglican Bishop of Gibraltar: 'We hear we are in your diocese.'

RICHARD CONSTABLE

Artist and great-grandson of John Constable

John Constable

(1776–1837)

The object in view in their production has been to display the phænomina of the chiaroscuro of nature, to mark some of its endless beauties and varieties, to point out its vast influence upon landscape, and to show its use and power as a medium of expression.

John Constable, Introduction to a series of mezzotints,
published towards the end of his life

'Constable's friend C. R. Leslie had this to say about him: "No man more earnestly desired to stand well with the world. He could not conceal his opinions of himself and of others; and what he said had too much point not to be repeated, and too much truth not to give offence. It it not then to be wondered at that some of his competitors hated him and most were afraid of him. He was opposed to all cant in art, to all that is merely suspicious and fashionable. With great docility he was an uncontrollable man!"

I feel this is a harsh view of Constable, as it must be said that those who were true friends would have "died" for him. He was generous and thoughtful to those worse off than himself. Samuel Lane, a fellow artist, was deaf and dumb, so Constable learned sign language in order to communicate with him. Through the Artists' Benevolent Fund he performed many kindnesses. He adored his children. His son Charles Golding read of his father's death in an English newspaper in Bombay when on a voyage to China. "O God," he wrote to his brother John, "how hard it seems that the Almighty should have snatched so kind and good a Father from us." An obituary in the *Ipswich Gazette* of 1837 ends: "In private life Mr Constable was much and deservedly esteemed. As an artist his place will not easily be supplied; and as a parent, friend and companion, his loss is irreparable".'

STEPHANIE COOK

Doctor and Olympic Pentathlon Gold Medallist

Eric Liddell

(1902–45)

I believe that God made me for a purpose – for China. But he also made me fast, and when I run I feel his pleasure. To give it up would be to hold him in contempt . . . to win is to honour him.

Eric Liddell

'Liddell never saw winning the Gold medal at the 1924 Olympics as the purpose of his life – his life service would be serving as a missionary in China. He has been one of my heroes and sources of inspiration because he gave his best to what he believed God had called him to do, and he used his talents to honour the Lord.'

ANTHONY KING

Age 9, Ash School, Somerset

Cristiano Ronaldo

(1985–)

Scoring goals in every match
being a good team mate.
Never grumbling about the referee,
playing for team and country,
performing at his best.

Anthony King

JILLY COOPER

Writer

Sir Walter Scott

(1771–1832)

Breathes there the man with soul so dead,
Who never to himself hath said,
This is my own, my native land.

Sir Walter Scott, from 'The Lay of the Last Minstrel', can.VI, i–ii

'Sir Walter Scott is one of my great heroes. He was not as good as writers such as Jane Austen but told wonderful, exciting stories. His poetry is romantic and moving.

I love Scott's sense of honour. He was in business with a bookseller called Ballantyne, who went spectacularly bankrupt. Scott spent the rest of his life writing to pay off debts of £114,000, a colossal sum in those days. The catastrophe seriously shortened his life.

Finally, he adored his dogs. His favourite was Camp, a Bulldog/Terrier cross, whose loyalty and intelligence made up for any lack of looks. When Camp died, Sir Walter buried him himself in the moonlight, and his daughter said she had never seen such a sad expression on anyone's face.'

Dr William Cope

Retired banker, lay reader in Yatton Keynall

Sir Anthony Cope

(1548/9–1617?)

O God, give us clean thoughts, clean words and clean hands. Help us to stand for the hard right against the easy wrong. Save us from habits that harm, teach us to work as hard and play as fairly in your sight as if all the world could see. Forgive us when we are unkind, and help us to forgive those who are unkind to us. Keep us ready to help others, even at some cost to ourselves; send us opportunities to do a little good every day and to grow more like Our Lord and Saviour Jesus Christ.

Sir Anthony Cope's prayer

'My ancestor Sir Anthony Cope was a puritanical MP for seven consecutive parliaments. He was imprisoned in the Tower in 1587 by Queen Elizabeth, for proposing that laws touching Church government should be made void, but was shortly released and was knighted by her in 1591. He lived in Hanwell Castle, and his name and escutcheon were engraved on Banbury cross when it was rebuilt in 1637.'

FRANCIS CORNISH
Retired ambassador to Israel

Siegfried Sassoon
(1886–1967)

I believe that this war ... has now become a war of aggression and conquest ... I am not protesting against the conduct of the war, but against the political errors and insincerities for which the fighting men are being sacrificed ... I believe that I may help to destroy the callous complacence with which the majority of those at home regard the continuance of agonies which they do not share, and which they have not sufficient imagination to realize.

Siegfried Sassoon, from a letter read out to Parliament
on 30 July 1917 and published in The Times the next day

'Sassoon's writings about the reality and futility of the First World War are extraordinarily intense and graphic, and it took huge courage to challenge not only the government and the military but also most of his own social class to stop it.

Earlier, he lived to the full the life of a young country gentleman – which largely vanished after the Great War; and he wrote about it as something to be preserved and defended, vividly and with infectious enthusiasm.'

¶ There is some lack of clarity about the origin of the quote. It may be from a letter to his Commanding Officer which was later included in the statement to Parliament and published in *The Times*. Sassoon could have been tried for treason for publicizing such a letter.

Retired diplomat, former Ambassador to Saudi Arabia

Revd Francis Kilvert

(1840–79)

Of all noxious animals, the most noxious is a tourist.

From *Francis Kilvert's Diary 1870–1879*, a selection edited
and introduced by William Plomer. From entry for 5 April 1870

'Revd Kilvert, as his diaries show, was a quiet, kind, decent, learned
man. He wrote mostly about nature and wildlife. Like him, I regard
tourism as a great danger, both to the environment and to the purity
and diversity of human culture.'

¶ In this passage Kilvert talks of seeing, from a mile away, Llanthony Abbey
ruins, '. . . the dim grey pile of building in the vale below, standing by the river-
side amongst its brilliant green meadow . . .', and seeing two tourists posturing
among the ruins, one pointing out with a stick to the other what he should
admire. Whether Kilvert had any premonition of the depredations that would
be caused by tourism, the editor does not know. There is now a pub and guest-
house in the Abbey ruins.

An example of Kilvert's lyrical writing is: 'A small and irreverent spider came
running swiftly towards me across the flat tombstone and scuttling over the
sacred words and memories with most indecent haste and levity. Here it was
very quiet and peaceful, nothing to disturb the stillness but the subdued village
voices and the cawing of the rooks nesting and brooding in the tops of the high
trees in the Castle clump. Somewhere near at hand I heard the innkeeper's voice
behind the church and across the brook giving orders to a workman about
planting some quick and privet' (from entry for 28 March 1871).

MARTIN CROSS

Olympic oarsman

≈

St Paul

(d. *c.* 65 CE)

Charity suffereth long, and is kind; charity envieth not; charity vaunteth not itself, is not puffed up, doth not behave itself unseemly, seeketh not her own, is not easily provoked, thinketh no evil; rejoiceth not in iniquity, but rejoiceth in the truth; beareth all things, believeth all things, hopeth all things, endureth all things.

Charity never faileth: but whether there be prophecies, they shall fail; whether there be tongues, they shall cease; whether there be knowledge, it shall vanish away.

1 Corinthians 13.4–8 (AV)

'St Paul is a hero because, though such a dynamic, brave and tough person with that thick skin necessary to endure all he faced on his travels, he was still able to write the most memorable description of love that exists. Our heroes reflect parts of us and qualities that we sometimes aspire to – if I could have Paul's energy, commitment and magnetism while retaining love and humility, then I would be truly blessed.'

JAMES CROWDEN

Poet

≈

St George

(d. *c.* 303)

St George for England, England's patron Saint to the rescue.
A land fit for heroes, fields clothed in green and gold
Wild daffodil and cowslips yellow, buttercups and meadow
    fescue,
Rich grazing laden with sprightly lambs and cattle bold

Roast beef. 'Arise Sir Loin', horseradish, red on white,
Playful language that holds the Globe within its grasp
The land of Shakespeare's crafted words, fine sonnets to delight
The Elizabethan Rose, oaken door upon its hasp.
Past deeds, like babbling brooks and glittering streams,
St George pre-occupied with damsel in distress, the next meal.
Crusader's chivalry, the answer to her frantic dreams,
Dragon brought to heel, the lance of hardened steel.
Oh spirit of England, warm in sheaves of April sunshine,
Let us make your beauty ours, orchard's blossom, spring divine.

James Crowden

'St George had very little to do with England. He was born in Palestine to a Christian family in the late third century. His father, from Cappadocia, was an officer in the Roman army. George joined the army, rose through the ranks and became an officer in the personal guard of the Emperor Diocletian. In 303 an edict was issued to persecute Christians. George admitted that he was Christian, was tortured and then decapitated on 23 April. He is venerated by the Eastern Orthodox Church. His cult came to England in the ninth century but reached its prominence during the crusades and was made popular by Shakespeare in *Henry V*. The dragon is a legend but adds colour to the maiden's cheeks.'

SUSAN CURTIS-BENNET

Retired civil servant

❧ ❧

John Stuart Mill

(1806–73)

Gender was . . . as entirely irrelevant to political rights as difference in height or in the colour of hair . . . a fresh social power would be acquired by giving freedom to one-half of the whole sum of human intellect . . .

Written by John Stuart Mill in 1859, taken from
John Stuart Mill: Victorian Firebrand by Richard Reeves

'John Stuart Mill is my hero without doubt. Gladstone called him the 'saint of rationalism'. Educated by his father to be an infant prodigy – he was taught Greek at the age of three – he later became one of the great Victorian reformers. An MP, he campaigned for reform of the House of Lords, the regulation of gambling, smoking and drinking, Irish land reform, a green environment, anti-racism – and most notably, for female suffrage.

Marriage, he said, should be based on equality, respectful partners, shared leadership and long-time friendship, a view not necessarily accepted at the time. Mill's campaign to secure votes for women was not fully realized until 1928. He thoroughly deserves his statue on the London Embankment.'

SIR COLIN DAVIS

Conductor

Nikos Kazantzakis

(1883–1957)

Take the old archer, Sun, in your caressing arms.
Don't leave him here alone, for see, the worms have come.
Their hidden jaws are munching at his entrails now!
Great Sun, flood down into his bowels, turn the worms
to thousands of huge, crimson, golden butterflies!
. . . let Death come . . .
to this lone man like a great Lord to knock with shame
on his five famous castle doors, and with great awe
plunder whatever dregs that in his sturdy body still
have not found time, in its great fight, to turn from flesh
and bone into pure spirit, lightning, joy and deeds.
The archer has fooled you Death, he's squandered all your
    goods,
melted down all the rusts and rots of his fond flesh
till they escaped you in pure spirit, and when you came
you'll find but trampled fires, embers, ash, and fleshly dross.

Nikos Kazantzakis, from *The Odyssey: A Modern Sequel*, Book xxiii

'To me, Kazantzakis was a major figure, though to some he was just a nuisance. Odysseus was Kazantzakis' hero, and Kazantzakis is mine; and this poem records, most movingly, the death of Odysseus.'

❡ Kazantzakis was born in Crete at the time of the island's revolt against the Ottoman Empire, causing his family to flee temporarily to Naxos. Writer, poet, philosopher, traveller and politician, he worked for the Greek government and for UNESCO. Films based on his books include *He Who Must Die*, *Zorba the Greek* and *The Last Temptation of Christ*.

Teresa de Bertodano
Freelance editor

Georges Vanier

(1888–1967)

The road of unity is the road of love: love of one's country and faith in its future will give new direction and purpose to our lives, lift us above our domestic quarrels, and unite us in dedication to the common good . . . I pray God that we may go forward hand in hand. We can't run the risk of this great country falling to pieces.

Georges Vanier, Governor General of Canada,
in one of the last speeches of his life

There are times when I feel very strong and sure of myself, especially in public . . . But there are other moments . . . when I am overwhelmed with a feeling of utter weakness and impotence. In these moments I say to Him, 'Jesus, I abandon myself to your merciful love', but I do not always say it with complete and utter confidence. Pray then, my beloved friend, that Jesus will give me the grace to believe, that He will give me total faith, that He will never forsake me. I am, as it were, like St Peter trying to walk on the surface of the water . . . I can only say, 'May His Will be done.'

Georges Vanier, from a letter to a Carmelite nun, 1959

'General Georges Vanier's career as soldier and diplomat culminated in his appointment age 72 as the first French Canadian Governor General of Canada in 1959. His life was a rare example of the successful co-existence of deep spirituality, supreme personal achievement and a happy marriage. In 1998 he was recognized by a distinguished panel as the hero with prime influence on the history of Canada.'

ESTHER DE WAAL

Writer

Father Christian de Chergé

(1937–96)

If the day comes, and it could be today, that I am a victim of the terrorism that seems to be engulfing all foreigners living in Algeria, I would like my community, my Church, and my family to remember that I have dedicated my life to God and Algeria . . . If the moment comes, I would hope to have the presence of mind, and the time, to ask for God's pardon and for that of my fellowman, and, at the same time, to pardon in all sincerity he who would attack me . . . My death will satisfy my most burning curiosity. At last, I will be able – if God pleases – to see the children of Islam as he sees them, illuminated in the glory of Christ, sharing in the gift of God's passion and of the Spirit, whose secret joy will always be to bring forth our common humanity amidst our differences . . . And to you, too, my friend of the last moment, who will not know what you are doing. Yes, for you, too, I wish this thank-you, this 'A-Dieu', whose image is in you also, that we may meet in heaven, like happy thieves, if it pleases God, our common Father. Amen! Insha Allah!

Father Christian de Chergé, written in anticipation of his death

'In the spring of 1996, armed men broke into a Trappist monastery in Algeria, Notre-Dame de l'Atlas in Tibhirine, known as a place of friendships between Christians and Muslims. Seven monks were taken hostage, pawns in murky terrorist negotiations. Two months later their severed heads were found in a tree; their bodies were never recovered. They became victims in a struggle that went wrong. They died because they refused to leave their Muslim friends who depended on them. Knowing the danger in which they lived, Father Christian de Chergé wrote this testament in anticipation of his death.'

GENERAL SIR JACK DEVERELL

Retired Army Officer

Duke of Wellington

(1769–1852)

The Lord's Prayer contains the sum total of religion and morals.

I mistrust the judgement of every man, in a case in which his own wishes are concerned.

Duke of Wellington

'The Duke of Wellington was a military innovator and reactionary, a man of great moral courage who, with a few words, could illuminate the most complex of issues. Though his private life was less than admirable, it is hard to identify a more successful British General. Of war he said, "Nothing except a battle lost can be half as melancholy as a battle won."

I particularly like this homely story about the Duke: The Duke once met a little boy, crying by the road. "Come now, that's no way for a young gentleman to behave. What's the matter?" he asked. "I have to go away to school tomorrow," sobbed the child, "and I'm worried about my pet toad. There's no one else to care for it and I shan't know how it is." Keen to ease the little chap's discomfort, the Duke promised to attend to the matter personally. After the boy had been at school for just over a week, he received a note: "Field Marshall the Duke of Wellington presents his compliments to Master —, and has the pleasure to inform him that his toad is well".'

POLLY DEVLIN

Journalist and writer

W. H. Auden

(1907–73)

From *Herman Melville*

. . . Evil is unspectacular and always human,
And shares our bed and eats at our own table,
And we are introduced to Goodness every day,
Even in drawing-rooms among a crowd of faults;
He has a name like Billy and is almost perfect
But wears a stammer like a decoration: . . .

W. H. Auden, from Collected Poems

'One of my heroes is W. H. Auden (all poets are heroes to me). I love his ironic lines "for poetry makes nothing happen" – when it so much does – for a start it moves our souls.'

COLIN DEXTER

Writer

Alfred Edward Housman

(1859–1936)

And I will friend you, if I may,
In the dark and cloudy day.

A. E. Housman, from A Shropshire Lad, Poem LXII

'Fourteen words, and all but one a monosyllable. A.E.H., that lonely old lugubrious soul, is not the greatest of the English poets, but from the age of 17 he has brought me more delight than any of them – and he has never let me down in times of disappointment (of which life is full). The couplet has been more treasured in my mental baggage than any other.'

THE REVD JAMES DICKIE

School Chaplain of Marlborough College

Marguerite Porete
(*c.* 1250/60–1310)

This book has been created by human knowledge and the human senses; and they know nothing about inner love, inner love from divine knowledge . . . God is greater than what is ever said, so everything one can say or write or think about Him is more like lying than speaking the truth.

Marguerite Porete, from the closing section of The Mirror of Simple Souls

'In 1306 Marguerite Porete was officially warned by Church authorities that her work was heretical. One of the taboos she had broken was writing the book in the language of ordinary people, rather than in Latin, and she was ordered not to circulate it again. Nevertheless she continued to do so. She was burned at the stake in 1310. As she died, the crowd was moved to tears by the calmness with which she faced her end. She went to the stake in silence, and died in silence.

Unlike other religious figures such as Joan of Arc, it is probable that Porete will never be recognized officially as a saint. This is partly due to her relative obscurity. Until 1946, it was not even known that she was the writer of *The Mirror of Simple Souls*.'

EMILY HIGGINS

Age 12, Long Sutton Primary School, Somerset

My Molly

You're like a sunbeam through a cloud
You're like a soothing piece of melody
Flying through the sky
You're like a sugary lemon cake
You're like a princess, pretty and kind
You're like a fizzy can of cold drink
Your face is like sunny Australia
You're a warm scarf that is
To warm me up when I get home
Your hair is a cosy bed of curls
You know you're not just any baby sister
You're my baby sister.

Emily Higgins

SIR PHILIP DOWSON

Architect

The Few

(1940)

The Universe is so vast and so ageless that the life of one man can
only be justified by the measure of his sacrifice.

From a letter by one of 'The Few'

'Rather than a single hero, I think often of the collective heroism of the
few pilots in 1940 whose impact made history. It was at that time
given voice by one in a letter to his mother in the event of his death.'

¶ The letter was written by Flying Officer Vivian Rosewarne and found by his
squadron leader among his possessions. He was reported missing in action on
31 May 1940. The letter was published at the request of his mother and his

squadron leader in *The Times* on 18 June 1940. He was finally declared dead on 23 December 1940. 'The Few' is in reference to the pilots of the Battle of Britain, and derived from Winston Churchill's words: 'Never in the field of human conflict was so much owed by so many to so few.'

THE REVD LADY DURAND

Rector of Kiltegan and Hacketstown group of parishes, Co. Wicklow, Republic of Ireland

Isaac of Nineveh

Seventh-century Kurdish Desert Father

A person of compassionate heart has a heart aflame for humankind, for the birds, the animals, for the devils, for every creature.

Isaac of Nineveh

'I think this is a needed message today, it is high time we greened our theology and included all God's creation in our love. In Revelation every creature praises God around his throne.'

¶ Nineveh, the most populous and oldest city in Assyria, lay on the east bank of the Tigris opposite modern Mosul (in northern Iraq).

HRH THE DUKE OF EDINBURGH

Prince Albert

(1819–61)

Very few men in modern times have made such a lasting and permanent mark in such a variety of fields, from the popularization of the Christmas tree to the saving of Cleopatra's Needle and its placing on the Thames Embankment; the spectacular revival of Cambridge University from medieval slumber to a world eminence it has never surrendered; the foundations of Imperial College were his work, as are the museums in South Kensington, the carved lions at the base of Nelson's Column in Trafalgar Square, the extension to the National Gallery and its glorious early Renaissance paintings whose purchase he inspired and of which 22 are his personal gift, the idea of the Royal Balcony on the façade of Buckingham Palace, the concept of the Model Village, and the inspiration for the Victoria Cross as the highest award for gallantry in battle, to be awarded regardless of rank. It is to him that we owe the tragically destroyed Crystal Palace, the great frescoes in the Royal Gallery in the Palace of Westminster, the exact manner in which the Koh-i-Noor diamond was cut, the abolition of duelling and the final defeat of slavery. And this is not the complete list of what he did for his adopted country.

From *Albert Prince Consort* by Robert Rhodes James

'My selection as a hero is Prince Albert, the Prince Consort. Apart from his quite remarkable achievements, he was my great-great-grandfather, and I have more reason than most to appreciate the challenges which he faced, as I occupy the same situation that he did. Indeed, I find myself occupying many of the same positions.'

❡ Among many of the positions held by both Prince Albert and the Duke of Edinburgh are President of the Commission for the Exhibition of 1851, Colonel of the Grenadier Guards, and President of the Royal Society of Arts. His Royal Highness is patron of over 770 charities and other organizations and holds over 30 senior appointments in the Services.

THE VERY REVD DR DAVID L. EDWARDS

Provost Emeritus, Southwark Cathedral, and former
Chaplain to the Speaker of the House of Commons

Albert Schweitzer

(1875–1965)

He comes to us as One unknown, without a name, as of old, by the lake-side He came to those men who knew him not. He speaks to us the same word: 'Follow thou me!' and sets us to the tasks which He has to fulfil for our time. He commands. And to those who obey him, whether they be wise or simple, He will reveal himself in the toils, the conflicts, the sufferings which they shall pass through in His fellowship, and, as an ineffable mystery, they shall learn in their own experience who He is.

Albert Schweitzer, from *The Quest of the Historical Jesus*

'This conclusion of Albert Schweitzer's *The Quest of the Historical Jesus* summed up for me the twin needs to be both completely honest and completely fascinated, and I used to quote it when I began to preach as an Anglican priest in the 1950s.'

Fred Edwards lvo

Voluntary worker, former Director of Social Work for Strathclyde, Chairman of Scottish Marriage Guidance, and President of Scottish Environment Link

Archie Craig

(1885–1985)

When we feel called upon to teach a lesson to any whose morals or manners offend us; we shall do well if first we reflect upon that scene in which the son of God knelt in the office of a slave, before Peter and Judas and the other moral mediocrities that made up the company of the Apostles.

Archie Craig

'What a corrective to any false pride which we may include in our personal baggage. How much it says about leader as servant, leader as pastor and building humility into strong leadership. Ever since hearing that reflection I have tried to incorporate the "foot washing" tradition in any aspect of leadership, management or governance that I have been required to discharge.'

¶ In the time of Christ, no male servant was obliged to undertake the task of washing feet, which was left to the most menial slave and was necessary in the dusty climate. This is St John's account: 'He riseth from supper, and laid aside his garments; and took a towel, and girded himself. After that he poureth water into a basin, and began to wash the disciples' feet, and to wipe them with the towel wherewith he was girded' (John 13.4–5, AV).

HYWEL TEIFI EDWARDS

Professor Emeritus, University of Wales, Swansea

Owain Glyndŵr

(c. 1354–1416)

These were the years of Owain Glyndŵr – Owen Glendower to the English – the most compelling of the emblematic heroes of the Welsh resistance . . . A prominent North Wales landowner, he rose against the English Crown between the years 1400 and 1410 and united almost all the Welsh behind him in a desperate guerrilla war of independence . . . The rebellion was defeated in the end . . . but Owain's wild and romantic explosion of resentment was to be remembered by Welsh people ever after as a glimpse of that other age which was embedded so deeply in their fancy . . . He is honoured still today, and his rising is idealized as the one grand moment of Welsh national completeness. Hard-headed historians see it in a different light, disparage its motives, deplore its effects, and present it as just another regional disruption in a period of distress and disaffection all over Europe. They are too late, though. Legend is far stronger than academic analysis, and Owain was long ago transmuted into a figure of myth. We see him to this day larger than life, the very image of the Welsh identity, slaughtering the English on bloody battlefields, undertaking adventures of picaresque effrontery, ranging the country north and south with his unconquerable Welsh guerrillas, *Plaint Owain*, Owain's children . . . Such is the power of historical suggestion. What became of Owain Glyndŵr nobody quite knows. In the best legendary way he disappeared from history. By now he is more than a man, he is an instinct. He is the Welshness in all Welshmen, whether they consciously acknowledge it or not. His is the spirit of their origins.

Jan Morris, from *The Matter of Wales*

'I have chosen Owain Glyndŵr, because for me he epitomizes heroism. He is embedded in Welsh hearts because of his high ideals and his determination to resist oppression. Despite the suffering endured by the people during his military campaigns, and though hunted high and low, he was never betrayed. His legend is imperishable.'

JOE WOOD
Age 10, Bishopsworth School, Bristol

Monkey Love Poem

Your fleas are so delicious,
Your hair so fair and fine,
And if I had the chance to,
I'd make sure you were mine.

Come with me my dear,
We'll swing among the trees.
No-one will disturb us
As we listen to the breeze.

We'll have dinner on the oak tree
With lady bugs, locusts and bees.
I'll feed you whatever you wish
Up in the tallest trees.

Joe Wood

STUART ELDON

Permanent Representative on the North Atlantic Council

Sérgio Vieira de Mello

(1948–2003)

A hero who dedicated his life to helping people in danger . . . Sérgio never shirked the most difficult assignments . . . where others saw obstacles or despair, he created options and solutions.

Colin Powell

'Sérgio Vieira de Mello, the former UN High Commissioner for Human Rights, was killed in an attack on the UN Headquarters in Baghdad in 2003. I knew him well and admired him in particular for his work in New York and in East Timor. Approachable, dedicated and effective, he was, as Kofi Annan said, "an outstanding servant of humanity".'

¶ Born in Rio de Janeiro, Vieira de Mello studied philosophy and humanities in Rio, then in Paris. He worked within the UN for refugees and human rights, had taken a lead role in the Lebanon, Rwanda, Kosovo, East Timor and Iraq, and had also worked in Bangladesh, Sudan, Cyprus, Mozambique, Peru and Yugoslavia.

PETER ELLIS

Barrister and retired civil servant

St Thomas More

(1478–1535)

And so was he by master Lieutenant brought out of the Tower and from thence led to the place of execution. Where going up the scaffold, which was so weak that it was ready to fall, he said merrily to Master Lieutenant, I pray you Master Lieutenant, see me safely up, and for my coming down let me shift for myself.

Then he earnestly entreated them to pray for the King so that

God would give him good counsel, and solemnly declared that he died the King's good servant but God's first.

From The Life of Sir Thomas More, Knight, Sometime Chancellor of England by William Roper, his son-in-law, written c. 1556

'This quotation illustrates the courage and ironic humour of Sir Thomas More (later recognized as Saint Thomas More). His steadfastness in the face of enormous pressure from the King and his advisers to go against his conscience was heroic. He had everything to live for: wealth, position, property and a loving family at Chelsea (who also could not understand his refusal to forgo his conscience and begged him to conform). His trial was a travesty of justice, and amounted to murder. The principal charge in the indictment was that, when asked to acknowledge that the King was the only and supreme head of the Church in England, he had refused to answer and had thus acted maliciously and treasonably.

He suffered most painfully for over one year in the Tower and with fears as to what awaited him. But he remained steadfast to the end, treating everyone with kindness, consideration and humour, refusing to appease the dictates of expediency.'

ALLAN EVANS

Former Scotland International football player

Ron Saunders

(1932–)

'Ron Saunders' management of Aston Villa in the Football League Championship opened the route to the European Cup. Alone with his team, his dour, almost military demeanour saw him disdainful of any opponent, though he remained invariably courteous when in public. His men faced many European greats but, having deliberately misread their names to his team immediately before the game, Saunders would screw the team sheet into a ball and throw it into a bin. In this way his players were convinced that they could beat anybody. For him, actions spoke louder than words.'

CHRISTOPHER EVANS

Retired headmaster

Robert Stephen Hawker

(1803–75)

Now, with twelve bodies still unfound . . . you will understand the
nervous wretched state in which we listen all day and all night for
those thrilling knocks at the door which announce the advent of the
Dead . . . A poor dissolving Carcase of Adam, seventeen days dead.

Revd Robert Stephen Hawker

'From 1834 until 1875 Robert Stephen Hawker was Vicar of Morwenstow, a remote parish on Cornwall's wild northern shore. At that
time any vessel caught close to its cliffs and jagged rocks with an on-
shore gale was doomed.

Overcoming his personal terrors, Hawker searched the beach
below his poet's driftwood hut for human remains, no matter how
scant, so that the seaman might be buried with dignity and Christian
hope. It is this work for the nameless dead that makes Hawker a hero.

Even in a county famous for eccentric incumbents, Revd Hawker
could appear decidedly odd. Diligent in his visiting, he strode about
his large parish with a palmer's staff, ample scarlet gloves and an
astonishing array of headgear, often accompanied by a pig. His
bishop tried to move him to a 'more appreciative' parish, but Hawker
stayed at Morwenstow. He restored the decayed church and built a
school and a substantial parsonage which he bequeathed to the
benefice. He is credited with inventing Harvest Festivals, sold
produce from his land to finance Christmas dinners for the poor and
composed the Cornish National Anthem ('And Shall Trelawney*
Die?'). He loved all animals including birds, fish and all God's creatures. Sometimes they accompanied him to worship and comprised
the congregation.

One of the Morwenstow church bells bears an apt inscription:

In Memoriam Robert Stephen Hawker, Vicar 1834 to 1875
Come to thy God in time:
Come to thy God at last.

'I would not be forgotten in this land,' he prayed. Nor should he be.'

¶ *Trelawney is the hero chosen by LADY MARY HOLBOROW.

THE REVD MEIRION EVANS
Past Archdruid of Wales

St David
(?–601)

On Sunday did David celebrate mass and preached to the people
. . . And having blessed everyone he then spoke thus: 'Lords,
brethren and sisters, be of good cheer, and keep your faith and your
belief, and cling to those little things of which you heard me speak
and my acts to which you were witnesses. And I will now walk the
way in which our fathers went. I bid you farewell,' said David, 'And
may your life on this earth be steadfast . . .'

And so on the first day of March did Jesus Christ take the soul of
David with great victory, joy and honour. After his fasting and his
thirst and his colds and his temperance and his charity and his
weariness and his troubles . . . and his concern for the world, then
did the angels take his soul and bring it to that place where there is
light without end, rest without labour, joy without sadness, abundance of all things that are good . . .

Rhigyfarch (*c.* 1000), *Vita Davidis*

'Dewi Sant – St David – a famous Celtic saint and Patron Saint of
Wales, founded a monastery at Vallis Rosina, in which valley stands
Saint David's Cathedral. Rhigyfarch wrote *Vita Davidis* in a Celtic
monastery at Llanbadarn Fawr in Ceredigion towards the end of the

eleventh century, some 500 years after David lived. St David's Day is celebrated on 1 March.'

¶ The Archdruid is the elected chief officer in the Gorsedd of Bards (allied to Wales's National Eisteddfod) and symbolic head of Welsh language and culture. The role bears no relationship to ancient druidism.

THE VERY REVD RICHARD EYRE
Dean Emeritus of Exeter Cathedral

Mother Janet Erskine Stuart
(1857–1914)

You know your life is all right, you know it *now*, don't you? And you trust God utterly and don't mind things being weird and unaccountable, do you? Because you know that He knows all about it, and will make it all right in the end. All crooked things will go right, and the word will come into the riddle, and the key into the puzzle, and we shall be so delighted to think that it was right all along and that we trusted Him when things were darkest and most incomprehensible.

From a letter by Mother Janet Erskine Stuart,
Superior General of the Order of the Sacred Heart (1911–14)

'I have long loved these words because they speak eloquently about the simultaneous darkness and joy of life with God. There is a gentle confidence about them. Mother Janet Erskine Stuart was a shy and much-loved person whose life was suffused by a quiet joy springing from her loving relationship with God. She was a great letter-writer and when writing to her nuns would sometimes employ hunting language to make her point, ". . . loosen your girths a little, Sister".'

U. A. FANTHORPE
Poet and writer

Julian of Norwich
(*c.* 1342–post-1416)

I saw for certain, both here and elsewhere, that before ever he made us, God loved us; and that his love has never been slackened, nor ever shall. In this love all his works have been done, and in this love he has made all things profitable to us; and in this love our life is everlasting. Our beginning was when we were made, but the love in which he made us never had beginning. In it we have our beginning.

Julian of Norwich, from *The Revelations of Divine Love*

'Julian of Norwich, though of humble stock was educated by nuns and became the first English woman prose writer using a blend of East Anglian and Northern dialects. She became an anchoress, withdrew to her cell to engage in a life of prayer and became supposedly dead to the world (her service of admission included, rather dauntingly, a Mass of the Dead) but her role was also to be useful to the people of Norwich who came to talk to her and seek her advice rather as if she were a kind of Citizen's Advice Bureau. After receiving the last rites during a near-terminal illness, she received revelations about the nature of God which she later set down as *The Revelations of Divine Love.*'

SIR ROBERT FFOLKES

Retired Development worker, former programme director for
Save the Children, Afghanistan

Shantideva

(Eighth century)

> As long as space endures,
> and as long as sentient beings exist,
> may I too remain
> to dispel the miseries of the world.

From a poem by Shantideva, Mahayana Buddhist Teacher

'Shantideva may seem an odd hero for a non-Buddhist, who knows no Sanskrit or classical Tibetan, to choose; but he speaks to everyone, encapsulating perfectly the imperative of love and kindness to all, in this one verse.

His poetry sings to anybody who knows the people of Tibet and the Himalayas. And it speaks of the importance of a life devoted to love and compassion. The spread of Buddhism from north India to Central Asia, Tibet and China, across the Himalayas, is one of the most fascinating stories of cultural transmission in history. And Shanitideva is one of those who inspired that cultural movement.

Before the advent of Buddhism the people of Central Asia, including the military empire in Tibet, were feared for their ferocity and success in war. The Buddhist teaching of compassion and universal love had, and still has, a profound impact on these societies, particularly in Tibet and most especially among the ordinary people.

Working now in the Mahayan Buddhist world, one becomes aware of the enduring influence for good of these teachings. I have seen many examples. A tough taxi-driver stops to remove grasshoppers from the road ahead, because he has been taught it is wrong to take life. Farmers in Ladakh pray at their harvest ritual for a better life for animals harmed during farm work. A young Tibetan insists that the Dalai Lama, the embodiment of compassion, cannot think only of Tibet, because 'he has to think of everyone'. The people who string flags above their houses or cairns on mountain passes do so, not to benefit themselves, but all sentient beings.'

TIMOTHY FFYTCHE
Ophthalmologist

Rudyard Kipling
(1865–1936)

The Curator nodded, wondering what would come next.

'So they made the triple trial of strength against all comers. And at the test of the Bow, our Lord first breaking that which they gave him, called for such a bow as none might bend. Thou knowest?'

'It is written. I have read.'

'And, overshooting all other marks, the arrow passed far and far beyond sight. At last it fell; and, where it touched earth, there broke out a stream which presently became a River, whose nature, by our Lord's beneficence, and that merit he acquired ere he freed himself, is that whoso bathes in it washes away all taint and speckle of sin'.

'So it is written,' said the Curator sadly.

The lama drew a long breath. 'Where is that River? Fountain of Wisdom, where fell the arrow?'

'Alas, my brother, I do not know,' said the Curator.

Rudyard Kipling, from *Kim*

'I am always moved by this little scene from *Kim*: a book that I return to again and again. In this meeting between two enlightened minds of different cultures – the lama and the Curator of the old Lahore Museum – Kipling frames one of the plots of a marvellous story, using an image that still has a spiritual resonance independent of any faith.'

Sir Winston Churchill

(1874–1965)

Democracy is the worst form of government except all those other forms that have been tried from time to time.

Winston Churchill, from a speech made in the House of Commons, 11 November 1947

'Winston Churchill has been a hero of mine since I was a child and still is today. He was a great decision-maker and always a wonderful wit.'

Matthew Fleming

Former cricketer for England and Captain of Kent County Cricket Club;
Director of family business

David Lloyd

(1947–)

I don't know what we would do without you, but we are going to find out.

David Lloyd

'David Lloyd, the England cricket manager, said this to me when he dropped me from the England team at Headingly in 1998. It taught me a huge lesson – bad news should be delivered directly, but with compassion.'

BILL FOGARTY

Dublin postman

St Patrick

(Mid- or late fourth century to *c.* 460 or 490)

Legend tells how King Laoghaire invited St Patrick to a conference at Tara on Easter night. His intention was to ambush Patrick and his eight companions; however, Patrick composed the hymn known as 'The Breastplate' or 'The Deer's Cry' as protection against the ambush. All the soldiers saw that night were eight deer and a fawn passing by.

> I bind unto myself today
>   The power of God to hold and lead,
> His eye to watch, his might to stay,
>   His ear to hearken to my need.
> The wisdom of my God to teach,
>   His hand to guide, his shield to ward;
> The word of God to give me speech,
>   His heavenly host to be my guard.

From the hymn 'I Bind Unto Myself Today', adapted from 'The Breastplate' by Cecil Frances Alexander (1818–95), wife of the Archbishop of Armagh

'St Patrick has shown us that no matter how lonely, depressed or abandoned we feel, with God in our lives he will guide us through.'

LIZZIE FORD

Age 10

St Nicholas

(Fourth century)

'My favourite saint is St Nicholas and my favourite hero is Santa Claus'.

Hendrika Foster
Art historian

William I, Count of Nassau
(known as 'The Silent'), Prince of Orange (1533–84)

*Je maintiendrey** [*sic*]; I shall maintain.
Saevis tranquillis in undis; quiet amidst billows.
Quotations from William's tomb, Nieuwe Kerk, Delft, Holland

'I admire William for his bravery, tenacity, military and political genius and devotion to the Dutch people. Born a minor European noble, wealth and responsibility was thrust upon William at the age of eleven, necessitating a move to the court in Brussels where he became companion and confidante to the Holy Roman Emperor Charles V. He staunchly defended the rights of the Dutch people against the fanatical Philip II of Spain, giving them his whole fortune and ultimately his life.

After his assassination, a contemporary mourned "Great is thy loss and greater will be thy misery O Flanders, for want of thy prince, who did guide thee with wisdom, love, policy and continual care for thy quietness."

William's qualities were reflected in the Dutch people who fought for justice and freedom from Spain for 80 years until their final victory in 1648. William is still thought of as the father of the Netherlands, and all following monarchs of the House of Orange have been buried with him, in Nieuwe Kerk, Delft. In the Second World War Queen Wilhelmina witnessed the invasion of her country by another malevolent foreign power. William was her hero, he is also mine.'

¶ *'Je maintiendrai' in modern French.

JOHN FRANCOME

National Hunt champion jockey and TV pundit

※ ※

My dad Norman

(1927–)

Make work a pleasure.

Norman Francome

LADY MARION FRASER

Chair of the Board of Christian Aid, 1990–97

※ ※

Mahatma Gandhi

(1869–1948)

Love is the strongest force the world possesses. And yet it is the humblest imaginable. The more efficient a force is, the more silent and subtle it is. Love is the subtlest force in the world.

When I read the Sermon on the Mount, especially such passages as 'Resist not evil', I was simply overjoyed and found my own opinion confirmed where I least expected it. The message of Jesus Christ, as I understand it, is contained in the Sermon on the Mount . . . which competes, almost on equal terms, with the Bhagavad Gita for the domination of my heart. It is that sermon which had endeared Jesus to me. The gentle figure of Christ, so patient, so kind, so loving, so full of forgiveness that he taught his followers not to retaliate when abused or struck but to turn the other cheek . . . it was a beautiful example, I thought, of the perfect man.

Mahatma Gandhi

'Gandhi has always fascinated me and I was so privileged to be able to visit his past in India and actually to meet one of his disciples who is . . . or was, as it is some years since I was there . . . still very involved with the peace movement. I have a very old schoolgirl's diary in which little of importance appears, but in large print I record the shock horror of Gandhi's assassination.'

¶ Mahatma, meaning great soul, was the name given to Gandhi as he won India's hearts. A devout Hindu, his peaceful actions led to the independence of India; but his generosity to others, particularly to Muslims, finally antagonized orthodox Hindus. He was shot by a fanatic on 30 January 1948. As he died, he uttered the name 'Rama'. Whoever recites the Ramayana or calls on Rama on their deathbed is freed from sin and attains heaven.

IAIN GALLOWAY

Retired management consultant

General Sir John Moore

(1761–1809)

The Burial of Sir John Moore after Corunna

Not a drum was heard, not a funeral note,
As his corpse to the rampart we hurried;
Not a soldier discharged his farewell shot
O'er the grave where our hero we buried.

We buried him darkly at dead of night,
The sods with our bayonets turning;
By the struggling moonbeam's misty light
And the lantern dimly burning.

Few and short were the prayers we said,
And we spoke not a word of sorrow;
But we steadfastly gazed on the face that was dead,
And we bitterly thought of the morrow.

We thought, as we hollow'd his narrow bed
And smoothed down his lonely pillow,

That the foe and the stranger would tread o'er his head,
And we far away on the billow!

Slowly and sadly we laid him down,
From the field of his fame fresh and gory;
We carved not a line, and we raised not a stone,
But we left him alone with his glory.

Charles Wolfe (1791–1823)

'When I was at the High School of Glasgow, the names of the four former pupils including that of General Sir John Moore were commemorated as the names of School Houses and were just names to me. It was not until I became a soldier that I came to recognize him as a brilliant officer and one whose humane treatment of subordinates and foes was of the highest order and way ahead of his time.

Moore was in command of the British forces in Spain during the Peninsular War when Napoleon arrived in Spain with 200,000 men. Moore then drew the French northwards while retreating to his embarkation ports of La Coruña and Vigo. He established a defensive position on hills outside the town, and was fatally injured at the Battle of Corunna. Throughout the several hours of his dying he remained conscious and composed, saying among his final words, "Remember me to your sister, Stanhope", referring to his friend Lady Hester Stanhope. He was buried in the ramparts of the town.

When the French took the town they built a monument over his grave. There are monuments in his honour in George Square Glasgow, St Paul's Cathedral, and at Shorncliffe camp near Folkestone.'

SIR JAMES GALWAY

Flautist

St John the Evangelist

(First century)

He that is without sin among you, let him first cast a stone at her.

John 8.7 (AV)

'Of all the evangelists, only John recounts the story of the woman taken in adultery. I think Christ's response is applicable to all of us, and is particularly relevant nowadays when no one seems willing to take responsibility for anything.'

¶ John 8.3–11 (AV): 'And the scribes and Pharisees brought unto him a woman taken in adultery; and when they had set her in the midst, they say unto him, Master, this woman was taken in adultery, in the very act. Now Moses in the law commanded us, that such should be stoned: but what sayest thou? This they said, tempting him, that they might have to accuse him. But Jesus stooped down, and with his finger wrote on the ground, as though he heard them not. So when they continued asking him, he lifted up himself, and said unto them, He that is without sin among you, let him first cast a stone at her. And again he stooped down, and wrote on the ground. And they which heard it, being convicted by their own conscience, went out one by one, beginning at the eldest, even unto the last: and Jesus was left alone, and the woman standing in the midst. When Jesus had lifted up himself, and saw none but the woman, he said unto her, Woman, where are those thine accusers? hath no man condemned thee? She said, No man, Lord. And Jesus said unto her, Neither do I condemn thee: go, and sin no more.'

GRAHAM GARRETT

Retired headmaster, musician and birdwatcher

St Bernadette of Lourdes

(1844–79)

It doesn't matter where we live as long as we live where we are.

St Bernadette of Lourdes

'This quotation encourages us to live life to the full no matter where it is and in whatever circumstances we find ourselves. Bernadette was a humble French girl who had visions of the Virgin Mary while she was tending the sheep. Her influence has enabled many thousands of pilgrims to find healing and peace after visiting her shrine in Lourdes, and we found our visit to this place of pilgrimage very moving.'

Thomas Sankara

(1949–87)

You cannot make big changes without also having a certain amount of madness. In this case it comes from non-conforming, having the courage to turn your back on the old formulas, the courage to invent the future. It is the crazy people of yesterday who enable us to live today with great clarity and understanding. I want to be like them. Let's dare to invent the future.

Thomas Sankara, from an interview in 1985,
with the Swiss journalist Jean-Phillippe Rapp

'The first time I came across Sankara's name was when I was travelling in West Africa in the early 1980s and saw people wearing T-shirts carrying his name and picture. A former President of Burkina Faso, he tackled corruption and fought for human and women's rights while implementing programmes for improved education, health, housing and reforestation. Internationally he denounced injustice, such as Nelson Mandela's imprisonment, the maltreatment of Native Americans in the USA, the dispossession of the Palestinian people, and the burden of Africa's foreign debt which he linked to the armament tragedy. Victoria Brittain, in her book *Thomas Sankara Speaks*, justly said, "the whole life of Thomas Sankara was a triumph . . . his courage and originality made him and Burkina Faso an inspiration . . . to so many Africans . . .".'

Leslie Garrett

Opera singer

Maria Grachvogel

'When complaining to the designer Maria Grachvogel that the dress she had made for me was too tight, and that I was finding it hard to breathe, Maria replied, "But darling, breathing is so last year".'

Peter George

Friend

The Virgin Mary

And a sword will pierce through your own soul also.

Luke 2.35 (RSV)

'My first heroine is Our Lady for she is Queen among those who "stand and wait". So often it is the women who carry a burden in this way. In his encyclical *Redemptoris Mater* Pope John Paul II wrote:

At the foot of the cross Mary shares through faith in the shocking mystery of this self-emptying. This is perhaps the deepest "kenosis"* of faith in human history. Through faith the Mother shares in the death of her Son, in his redeeming death; but in contrast with the faith of the disciples who fled, hers was far more enlightened. On Golgotha, Jesus through the cross definitively confirmed that he was the "sign of contradiction" forecast by Simeon. At the same time, there were also fulfilled on Golgotha the words which Simeon had addressed to Mary: "Yea, a sword shall pierce through thy own soul also".'

❡ *Kenosis: Christ's voluntary renunciation of certain divine attributes in order to identify himself with humankind.

ALAN GIBBS

Conductor and composer

Gustav Holst

(1874–1934)

Every artist ought to pray that he may not be 'a success'. If he's a failure he stands a good chance of concentrating upon the best work of which he's capable.

Gustav Holst, remark made to Clifford Bax*

'Holst, far from living in an ivory tower, devoted much of his energy to training young and adult amateurs. A former pupil described him as totally unpretentious and said that, when success finally came to him with *The Planets* and *The Hymn of Jesus*, his embarrassment was plain to see.'

❡ *Quoted by Bax in *Inland Far: A Book of Thoughts and Impressions.*

SIR NICHOLAS GOODISON
Banker and author

※ ※

Socrates

(469–399 BC)

Socrates walked about, and presently, saying that his legs were heavy, lay down on his back – that was what the man recommended. The man (he was the same one who had administered the poison) kept his hand upon Socrates, and after a little while examined his feet and legs; then pinched his foot hard and asked if he felt it. Socrates said no. Then he did the same to his legs; and moving gradually upwards in this way let us see that he was getting cold and numb. Presently he felt him again and said that when it reached the heart, Socrates would be gone.

The coldness was spreading about as far as his waist when Socrates uncovered his face – for he had covered it up – and said (they were his last words): 'Crito, we ought to offer a cock to Asclepius. See to it, and don't forget.'

'No, it shall be done,' said Crito. 'Are you sure that there is nothing else?'

Socrates made no reply to this question, but after a little while he stirred; and when the man uncovered him, his eyes were fixed. When Crito saw this, he closed the mouth and eyes.

Such, Echecrates, was the end of our comrade, who was, we may fairly say, of all those whom we knew in our time, the bravest and also the wisest and most upright man.

Plato (*c.* 428–347 BC), from *Phaedo*

'This is the passage at the end of Plato's *Phaedo* describing the death of Socrates. He has been condemned to death by the Athenian court after a trumped-up trial on charges of impiety and corrupting the young, showing that extremism is nothing new. He has drunk the poison in the company of his friends. His pious reference to Asclepius, the god of healing, ironically implies that death is the cure for life. Socrates has had a profound influence on the development of western thought and ethics, chiefly through the writings of Plato.'

ADAM GOSLING

World Champion, Etchell Racing Dinghies 1996

❦

Ernest Shackleton

(1874–1922)

Difficulties are just things to overcome, after all.

Ernest Shackleton

'Ernest Shackleton was the type of explorer who, when things were not going his way, found the solution. His way of leadership and determination still augurs for a good example today and, for those of us at sea in modern boats with modern equipment, puts us in our place when things are a little uncomfortable.'

DR DESMOND GRAVES

Retired management teacher

❦

Hildegard von Bingen

(1098–1179)

Just as the power of God, extending everywhere surrounds all things without encountering any resistance, so too the rationality of man has the great ability to sound through living voices . . . Even David demonstrates this in the music of his prophecy . . . So it is that even you – a poor weak-natured little woman – hear, in music, the sound of fiery ardour in the virgin's blush, in the embracing word of the budding twig; the sound of keenness from the living lights that shine in the celestial city; . . . But you also hear a sound like the voice of a great throng, resounding in harmony in the complaints of those recalled to the same steps. For music not only rejoices in the unanimity of exultation of those who bravely persevere along the path of righteousness. It also exults in the concord of reviving those who have fallen away from the path of justice and are lifted up at last to blessedness. For even the good shepherd joyfully led back to the flock the sheep that had been lost.

Hildegard von Bingen, from *Scivias* (*Know the Ways of the Lord*),
Vol. III, Ch. 13

'Social entrepreneur, guru, know-all, alternative deputy abbess (she was not allowed to preside, as nuns were not allowed to administer the sacraments), and control freak, she is credited with more or less inventing church music in the twelfth century. She got into trouble with the establishment because she allowed her nuns to wear long hair and jewellery. A woman for our times.'

LUCINDA GREEN
Olympic equestrian and author

Anonymous

Life is full of shadows, but the sunshine makes them all.

'I don't know the author of this quotation, but they have certainly inspired me by what they said.'

Sir Peter Hall

Theatre opera and film director

Harley Granville Barker

(1877–1946)

A play, in fact, as we find it written, is a magic spell; and even the magician cannot always foresee the full effect of it.

Harley Granville Barker, from his preface to *Cymbeline*

'Harley Granville Barker, theatre director, actor, producer, playwright and author, has been a key influence in my professional life from an early age. He was one of the most profound and subtle dramatists we had, until Samuel Beckett inaugurated the golden age of twenti-eth-century drama. But he remains in many ways Britain's unsung dramatist. He was clearly our first great theatre director, and his *Prefaces to Shakespeare* remains the most practical guide among all the countless books on the over-scrutinized subject. Without Granville Barker's inspiration there probably would not be a National Theatre. He articulated what it could do and campaigned for its existence throughout his life. He has been a beacon for a whole generation of theatre directors.'

Robin Hamilton

Nature conservationist

Charles Darwin

(1809–82)

There is grandeur in this view of life, with its several powers, having been originally breathed into a few forms or into one; and that, whilst this planet has gone cycling on according to the fixed law of gravity, from so simple a beginning endless forms most beautiful and most wonderful have been, and are being evolved.

Charles Darwin, from *On the Origin of Species by Means of Natural Selection*

'Charles Darwin, that brilliant and meticulous scientist, is a hero of mine because of his genius in deducing the truth of evolution by natural selection, and his courage in publishing his great work *On the Origin of Species* . . . despite the anger and ridicule that he knew would initially greet it. The book's unemotional prose, some of the driest in the English language, was hated by those who cherished the beautiful myth of the Creation. But its magnificent concluding sentence clearly shows that Darwin, a kind and gentle man, did not lack emotion and was deeply moved by the grandeur and beauty of what he had discovered.'

❡ These words of Charles Darwin's were also chosen by HUGH TRIPP, Somerset wine and cider maker, who added that 'Darwin created the defining moment for mankind: awareness of our time and place in the world.'

ROBERT HAMILTON

Former Australian Ambassador to Mexico, Cuba and Central America

❧ ❧

Arthur Boyd

(1920–1999)

It has fallen to people like Arthur to define what it is to be Australian on canvas and to let us understand that we're not Europeans anymore, that we're not anything other than Australians.

Said by former Prime Minister of Australia, Paul Keating, on the death of Boyd

'Arthur Boyd was born into a family of artists and writers, and became one of Australia's best-known artists. His early works drew on his wartime experiences and his travels through central Australia and Aboriginal communities and was inspired by the Australian landscape and the Bible. In 1993, the Boyd family donated his beloved property, on the Shoalhaven River, to the Australian people for use as an artists' retreat and gallery.'

SIR DAVID HARE
Playwright

Studs Terkel
(1912–)

It's dog eat dog. But we're not dogs, that's the problem.

Studs Terkel

'Studs Terkel is a great Chicago author and interviewer, and this quotation tells you everything you need to know about western values of the last 30 years.'

PETER HARFORD
Writer

Dante
(1265–1321)

Dico che quando ella apparia da parte alcuna, per la speranza de la mirabile salute nullo nemico mi rimanea, anzi mi giugnea una fiamma di caritate, la quale mi facea perdonare a chiunque m'avesse offeso; e chi allora m'avesse domandato di cosa alcuna, la mia risponsione sarebbe stata solamente 'Amore', con viso vestito d'umilitade.

I say that whenever she appeared in any place, through the hope of her miraculous salutation there remained no enemy for me – a flame of charity burst in me which caused me to forgive everyone who had offended me. And to anyone who at such time would ask me anything my reply would simply be: 'Love', my face clothed in humility.

Dante Alighieri, from *Vita Nuova*, chapter 11, translated by Vittorio Montemaggi

'The great Italian poet Dante reveals his love for Beatrice. It was "love at first sight" of the girl from Florence who died not more than 24 years old. Dante would love her always. Beatrice became that most moving symbol of salutation and of God's manifestation without whose image *The Divine Comedy* would most assuredly have been a different affair. The quotation is an incisive expression of pure love, untrammelled by life's complications. For me, the noble Dante's words remain significant. The purer the love in our hearts, then perhaps the simpler and happier our lives would be.'

Dr Tarek H. A. Hassan

Emeritus Professor of Medicine, Ashar University, Cairo

Mahatma Gandhi

(1869–1948)

What difference does it make to the dead, the orphans and the homeless, whether the mad destruction is wrought under the name of totalitarianism or the holy name of liberty or democracy?

Mahatma Gandhi

'My favourite greats are Gandhi and Mozart and some of the sublime verses from the Koran that transmit a completely different meaning from that generally perceived in the west.'

Sir Max Hastings

James Graham, Marquis of Montrose

(1612–50)

He either fears his fate too much
Or his deserts are small

That does not put it to the touch
To win or lose it all.

'When Charles I's fortunes were already all but lost in the English Civil War, in 1644 James Graham, Marquis of Montrose, rode into Scotland with just two companions, raised a wild little army of Irish and Highland clansmen for the King and led them to a series of stunning victories against overwhelmingly superior Covenanting armies. A brilliant commander as well as an unflinching champion of lost causes, it was said that Montrose went gaily to his doom, "as to meet a bride". He has been foremost in my own pantheon since I retraced his legendary winter march through the snows from Blair Atholl to Inverary in January 1976, while writing his biography. His achievements represent a marvel of romance, courage and initiative.'

His Hon. Richard O. Havery

Former judge of the technology and construction court, London

Sir Isaac Newton

(1643–1727)

If I have seen further, it is by standing on the shoulders of giants.

Sir Isaac Newton, from a letter to Robert Hooke, 5 February 1675/76

'My great hero is Sir Isaac Newton. I admire him for his supreme intellectual achievement in discovering the theory of gravity, explaining the tides, the notion of motion, the orbs of the planets and the procession of the equinoxes. He was described (modestly) by that great mathematician Gauss as the greatest mathematician since Archimedes.

I consider the letter to be gracious and that he wished to make it clear that he stood on the shoulders of Galileo and Descartes, as was the case, and indeed that some of the knowledge had come from the ancient Greeks and Romans. Who knows what knowledge was lost when the library at Alexandria was destroyed?'

¶ The context of Newton's letter to his rival Hooke about his work on light is 'What Descartes did was a good step. You have added much in several ways, and especially in taking the colours of thin plates into philosophical consideration. If I have seen a little further it is by standing on the shoulders of giants.' Newton would have known Robert Burton's popular book of the time, *Anatomy of Melancholy*, and the quotation in it 'Pygmies placed on the shoulders of giants see more than the giants themselves'.

LADY HEATH

Yachtswoman and countrywoman

Robert Louis Stevenson

(1850–94) and the 'Lighthouse Stevensons'

Happiness Prayer

Grant to us, O Lord, the royalty of inward happiness,
and the serenity which comes from living close to thee.
Daily renew in us the sense of joy,
and let the eternal spirit of the Father dwell in our souls and
    bodies,
filling every corner of our hearts with light and grace;
so that, bearing about with us the infection of good courage,
we may be diffusers of life,
and may meet all ills and cross accidents with gallant and
    high-hearted happiness,
giving thee thanks always for all things.

Robert Louis Stevenson

'I heard this poem at a memorial service and was surprised to discover that it was written by Robert Louis Stevenson; I had imagined it to be earlier. I feel it encapsulates the appreciation and gratitude we should aspire to show in our gift of life.

While I admire the works of Robert Louis, as a sailor my real heroes are his family, the 'Lighthouse Stevensons', who built 14 towering structures in the most inhospitable places imaginable around the Scottish coast – majestic feats of engineering and endurance – for which I have often given thanks. Robert wrote, "Whenever I smell salt water I know I am not far from the works of my ancestors".'

PADDY HEAZELL

Retired headmaster

Sir Peter Ustinov

(1921–2004)

I was irrevocably betrothed to laughter, the sound of which has always seemed to me to be the most civilised music in the world.

Sir Peter Ustinov, quoted from an interview in old age

'Described as a true Renaissance Man of the twentieth century, Ustinov was uniquely multi-talented. Playwright, actor, producer/director, author and, above all, raconteur, he was a man of rare humanity and breadth of culture. His family background qualified him to be the ideal UNICEF Goodwill Ambassador. He once confessed: "It's difficult for me to feel British . . . I rather think of myself as ethnically filthy – and proud of it."

He was born in north London and attended a great English public school from which he alleges he received a report: "He shows great originality which must be curbed at all costs." His gift for languages and mimicry and his acute eye for the comic and curious made him an unsurpassed conversationalist. He was knighted in 1990, as much as anything for making people laugh and the world a better place. A final achievement was his Institute for Combating Prejudice.'

ELIZABETH HEIM

Grandmother

※ ⁂

Sir Francis Drake

(1540?–95)

My masters, I must have it left. I must have the gentleman to hale
and drawe with the mariner, and the mariner with the gentleman
... I would know him that would refuse to hale on a rope, but I
know there are none such here ... are we not of one company?

Sir Francis, from a speech made to his discontented crews on 11 August 1578, at
Port St Julian, South America, before the passage round Cape Horn

'Drake created, in an age where the Queen's Navy was sharply divided
into the sailors who worked the ship and the gentlemen who commanded it, camaraderie and fellowship where birth mattered less
than the matter in hand.

   Equality of obligation at this level was not to be generally understood for another 50 years. Resourcefulness, courage, imagination,
innovation and an indomitable will inspire admiration. Add to this a
force of concise expression, and you have a man to be considered
among the world's great commanders.'

PAUL HEIM

Barrister

※ ✤

Moses Maimonides

(1135–1204)

It is not enough to give assistance to those who are in need of our help; we must look after their interests, be kind to them.

He shall dwell among thee . . . where it listeth him; thou shalt not vex him.

> Moses Maimonides, with reference to the Old Testament,
> and on the obligation to the stranger, from the *Guide for the Perplexed*

'Maimonides was recognized in his time as a great philosopher and sage, a man who in his writings brought together ancient Jewish thought and Aristotelian principles. As a physician he similarly considered the health of the mind with the health of the body. "Exercise each day to breathlessness" was one of his many precepts which have endured to modern times.

He preached tolerance, moderation, charity, honesty and right behaviour. As a victim of persecution himself, writing later in the tranquillity of Cairo, he recalled Old Testament obligations. His *Guide for the Perplexed* is read to this day, and is valued for its modernity, clarity and abiding humanity.'

❡ Moses Maimonides was also chosen by the RT HON. THE LADY NEUBERGER, writer and politician, who selected a quotation about his grading of charitable giving, of which there are several: 'The highest level, above which there is no other, is to strengthen the reputation of another person by giving him a present or a loan, by taking him into partnership, or by finding him a job in order to strengthen his hand so that he no longer needs to beg for alms . . . and below this is the person who gives alms unwillingly' (Moses Maimonides, from his codification of Jewish Law, *Mishneh Torah – Hilchot Mat'not Ani'im*, 10:7 ff. Lady Neuberger says: 'I like this piece by Maimonides, the great doctor, Rabbi and polymath because it suggests that the giving of charity is not a matter of choice, but obligation, and that there is a religious duty to do it well.'

John Hewer

Volunteer, hospital transport driver

❦

Frankie Dettori

(1970–)

'I have chosen Frankie Dettori, champion jockey, because of his smile, and his obvious delight, and often surprise when he wins, which is frequently. His pleasure is infectious, and makes everyone feel better.'

Robert Hobhouse

Teacher

❦

His Holiness the Dalai Lama

(1935–)

The only way to be happy is to be kind.

The Dalai Lama

'It is embarrassing to nominate as my "hero" someone as well known as His Holiness the Dalai Lama. This is as bad as Catholics claiming the Pope as their hero. The leader of the Tibetan Buddhists has won the Nobel Peace Prize for his non-violent resistance to the Chinese, but it is not for his political work that he is my pick. In fact, making known to the world what the Chinese are doing is merely him doing his job.

Where he has gone way beyond his job is trying to build bridges between Tibetan Buddhism and other faiths. I am particularly fond of this idea of his, and think it is a perfect connection between Buddhist thought and Christian beliefs. The background theology is different (and in Buddhism it is very complicated, involving not wishing for your own happiness at all; i.e., the only way to be happy is to not to work for your own happiness), but the result is the same.'

LADY MARY HOLBOROW, JP

Lord Lieutenant of Cornwall

※ ⚮

The Rt Revd Sir Jonathan Trelawny

(1650–1721)

From *The Song of the Western Men: Trelawny*

> And shall Trelawny die?
> Here's twenty thousand Cornish men
> Will know the reason why!

Revd R. S. Hawker (1803?–75).
These three lines from verse 2 of the song are traditional

Forasmuch as the mercies received from Almighty God do call for suitable returns of gratitude on our part, and yet all our goods are nothing until Him who is all sufficient; and therefore the best way of expressing our thankfulness to Him for the good things we have received of Him is by doing good to others . . .

Trelawny's prayer

'Bishop Trelawny was born in Pelynt, a member of this ancient family who settled in Cornwall in Saxon times. He was ordained and also inherited his father's baronetcy in 1673. A priest and a soldier, he organized the defence of Cornwall during Monmouth's rebellion and was then made Bishop of Bristol. Though intensely loyal to the Crown, in 1688, with six other bishops, he petitioned King James II against his Declaration of Indulgence. They were imprisoned in the Tower and tried for treason. Trelawny recorded his own words at the trial:

"Struck with that word rebellion I fell on my knees and in heate and confusion spoke thus: 'Rebellions Sir! I beseech your Majesty do not say so hard a thing of us, for God's sake do not believe we are or can be guilty of a rebellion. It is impossible for me or my family to be guilty of rebellion. Your Majesty cannot but remember that you sent me to quell Monmouth's rebellion and I am ready to do what I can to quell another. We will do our duty to Your Majesty to the utmost in every thing that does not interfere with our duty to God'."

"Trelawny", the Cornish national song, is sung lustily by hundreds at sporting events – a moving experience to hear, especially when Cornwall won the Rugby finals at Twickenham.'

¶ Revd R. S. Hawker was also chosen by CHRISTOPHER EVANS.

JANE HOLDERNESS-RODDAM (JANE BULLEN)
Olympic Team Gold Medallist and Badminton Horse Trials winner

Rudyard Kipling
(1865–1936)

If

If you can keep your head when all about you
Are losing theirs and blaming it on you,
If you can trust yourself when all men doubt you,
But make allowance for their doubting too;
If you can wait and not be tired by waiting,
Or being lied about, don't deal in lies,
Or being hated, don't give way to hating,
And yet don't look too good, nor talk too wise:

. . .

If you can fill the unforgiving minute
With sixty seconds' worth of distance run,
Yours is the Earth and everything that's in it,
And – which is more – you'll be a Man, my son!

Rudyard Kipling

'The person who has most influenced my life, outside my own family, is undoubtedly Rudyard Kipling. Brought up to read *The Jungle Book* which taught me so much understanding, I was then, at 18, told to stick to the words from his poem "If" – and what a wonderful influence and support these have been to me through thick and thin.

The words in his poem are extraordinary, in that they have and do come into every eventuality in one's life. Kipling's words have helped me time and time again and, for that, he has to be my "Favourite Hero" and is someone to whom I feel eternally grateful.'

ADRIAN HOUSE

Writer

St Francis of Assisi

(1181–1226)

The Little Flowers of St Francis describes how the friars were being driven to distraction by an increasingly offensive leper. They managed to put up with his constant abuse for failing to look after him with proper compassion, but they couldn't stand his blasphemy when he began to vilify Christ. They therefore turned to Francis for help, who went to see the leper and gave him his usual greeting, 'Peace be with you.'

'What peace?' the leper asked. 'God hasn't only taken away my peace and everything else worth having, but has also left me rotten and stinking.' When Francis urged patience, he began ranting about the friars.

After praying for the man, Francis went back to the leper and offered to do whatever he asked.

'Wash me,' he answered, 'because I smell so awful and I can't bear myself.'

Francis therefore undressed and washed him in warm water scented with herbs, and wherever he swabbed the flesh it started to heal. As the leper's body mended so did his soul, and when he was entirely recovered he apologised and did penance for cursing God and the friars.

By then, Francis was 'very far away because he desired to flee from every glory'.

From *Francis of Assisi* by Adrian House

'When writing about Francis' life I felt that no story conveyed his essence better than this one, handed down by several generations of friars and included in *The Little Flowers*. During the thirteenth century the example of Francis' unfailing compassion and humility saved the degenerating Church from disintegration and has inspired his Order ever since. In a strange testament, the world-famous atheist scholar Ernest Renan wrote: "After Jesus, Francis of Assisi has been the only perfect Christian".'

LORD HOYLE OF WARRINGTON

Chairman of Warrington Wolves Rugby League Football Club

John F. Kennedy

(1917–63)

When power narrows the area of man's concern, poetry reminds him of the richness and diversity of his existence.

When power corrupts, poetry cleanses.

For art establishes the basic human truths which must serve as the roadstones of our judgement.

President John F. Kennedy, from a speech made on 26 October 1963

'I believe that if he had not been so cruelly assassinated, John F. Kennedy would have continued as a great statesman and leader who would have made a major contribution to ending the Cold War with Russia.'

TREVOR HUDSON

General Practitioner

Florence Nightingale

(1820–1910)

I can never forget. I stand at the altar of the murdered men, and while I live I will fight their cause.

From the private notes of Florence Nightingale

It seemed an endless walk as we passed by, the silence was profound – not a moan or a cry. Miss Nightingale carried her lantern which she would set down before she bent over one of the patients.

A nurse accompanying Miss Nightingale

'In 1854 Florence Nightingale, aged 34, arrived with a team of 38 nurses in the Crimea. Even before the fighting started, cholera had taken its toll, and supplies to the soldiers were disorganized and inadequate. The converted Turkish barracks in Scutari had become a death trap. No beds, no hospital equipment, and primitive sanitation. Using funds given by public appeal and her own efforts, Florence bought supplies, set up a kitchen, cleaned the halls, and reopened and equipped a whole disused wing of the barracks.

At first Florence Nightingale had to fight for authority over her nurses – no work could be done unless authorized by a doctor. However, after the Battle of Inkerman casualties were so numerous that suspicion vanished and her work was authorized. At one time she estimated there were four miles of patients, with 18 inches between each. The duty surgeon was so busy inspecting and form-filling that there was no time for patient care.

She never let a man in her care die alone and estimated that, during one winter, she witnessed 2,000 deaths. She attended every severe case without regard for her own contagion, and kept meticulous records. She begged for improved sanitation until finally a commission from Britain arrived. In two weeks they removed 550 handcarts and baskets of filth, buried 26 dead animals, and cleaned the water supply. The mortality rate dropped from 20 per cent to 2 per cent.

She remained after the war to continue improvements, but as the crisis of war passed, opposition to her work gathered pace. There was petty jealousy, misrepresentation and open treachery. Exhausted physically and mentally, she was overcome by a sense of failure and returned home unnoticed. However, Queen Victoria read her reports, summoned her to Balmoral, and instituted a Royal Commission of Enquiry in which Florence demonstrated that mortality in Army barracks was over twice that in the local population. "Our soldiers enlist to death in the barracks and 1,500 are as certainly killed as if drawn up on Salisbury Plain and shot."

She set up a training school for nurses and her reforms revolutionized hospital practice worldwide. When Florence died, aged 90, there was, at her request, no public mourning. She is buried in her family churchyard in East Wellow, near Romsey, Hampshire. The inscription on her headstone reads simply: F.N. Born 1820 Died 1910.'

The Rt Hon. Lord Hurd of Westwell

Statesman

~~~ ~~~

Sir Robert Peel

(1788–1850)

I shall leave a name execrated by every monopolist . . . but it may be that I shall leave a name sometimes remembered with expressions of goodwill in the abodes of those whose lot it is to labour and to earn their daily bread by the sweat of their brow, when they shall recruit their exhausted strength with abundant and untaxed food, the sweeter because it is no longer leavened by a sense of injustice.

Sir Robert Peel, from a speech in 1846

'It is with these words that Robert Peel ended the fierce campaign for the Repeal of the Corn Laws. This was a decision which he took at great personal cost to himself because of his overwhelming concern that only this measure could remedy the acute poverty in our industrial towns and cities. It is a classic example of political courage which I have often admired.'

¶ Sir Robert Peel was also chosen by IVOR LUCAS, former Ambassador in Damascus, who chose the same quote and wrote: 'Peel has always been my favourite statesman because he had the courage to change his mind on matters of conscience (an earlier issue was that of Catholic Emancipation) despite the career consequences. Sir Robert Peel was described by one historian as "the only English statesman on whose death the poor have wept in the streets".'

Peel's Tory Party relied heavily on the votes of the landowners who had invested much during the Napoleonic Wars to improve their land and provide corn for the nation. The Corn Laws protected them against the import of cheap corn which peace had made a possibility.

The new industrialists were pressing for free trade and for a healthier workforce, meanwhile the poor faced misery.

Disraeli attacked Peel for betraying his own party but Peel had seen the greater good. The anti-Corn Law League was headed up by Cobden and Bright, the former dying young as a result of the exertions exacted by this cause.

LIEUTENANT COLONEL IAN HYWELL-JONES

Project Co-ordinator, The Victoria Cross and George Cross research project

Field Marshall Lord Wavell

(1883–1950)

Arab Love Song

The hunched camels of the night
Trouble the bright
And the silver waters of the moon.
The maiden of the morn will soon
Through heaven stray and sing,
Star gathering.

Now that the dark about our love is strewn,
Light of my dark, blood of my heart, O come!
And the night will catch her breath up and be dumb.

Leave thy father, leave thy mother
And thy brother;
Leave the black tents of thy tribe apart!
Am I not thy father and thy brother,
And thy mother?
And thou-what needest with thy tribe's black tents
Who hast the red pavilion of my heart?

Francis Thompson (1859–1907)

'Wavell was a remarkable soldier, statesman and scholar. This poem was published in his anthology *Other Men's Flowers*, and the Memorial Edition I bought in 1952 (the year in which I was commissioned) has never been far from me since.'

¶ Wavell had a phenomenal memory, and would recite the poems, most of which he knew by heart. He had a great belief in the inspiration of poetry towards courage and vision. The poem quoted was one of his own favourites.

Dr Denise Inge

Writer

Thomas Traherne

(1637?–74)

It was His wisdom made you need the Sun. It was His goodness made you need the sea. Be sensible to what you need, or enjoy neither. Consider how much you need them, for thence they derive their value. Suppose the sun were extinguished: or the sea were dry. There would be no light, no beauty, no warmth, no fruits, no flowers, no pleasant gardens, feasts or prospects, no wine, no oil, no bread, no life, no motion. Would you not give all the gold and silver in the Indies for such a treasure? Prize it now you have it, at that rate, and you shall be a grateful creature: Nay, you shall be a Divine and Heavenly person. For they in Heaven do prize blessings when they have them. They in Earth when they have them prize them not, they in Hell prize them when they have them not.

Thomas Traherne, from *The Centuries of Meditations*, Century I, 46

❡ Thomas Traherne was also chosen by HUGH PARRY, Adult Education Tutor, who selected this passage in the original English.

I was a little Stranger which at my Enterance into the World was Saluted and Surrounded with innumerable Joys. My Knowledg was Divine: I knew by Intuition those things which since my Apostasie, I Collected again, by the Highest Reason. My very Ignorance was Advantageous. I seemed as one brought into the Estate of Innocence. All Things were Spotles and Pure and Glorious: yea, and infinitely mine, and Joyfull and Precious . . . All Time was Eternity, and a Perpetual Sabbath. Is it not Strange, that an Infant should be Heir of the World, and see those Mysteries which the Books of the Learned never unfold?

Thomas Traherne, from *The Centuries of Meditations*, Century III, 2

'Traherne was a sort of "holy fool", but more holy than fool, and the world would do well to cherish his rare kind. In an age of paranoia, bigotry and life-denial, he found a Christian philosophy which his contemporaries were too blinkered to see. Goodness and happiness were as real to him as they have ever been to anybody: sin, death and punishment were almost off his radar. I don't know if he was right, but I wish he were.'

LADY INNES OF EDINGIGHT

Prison visitor

❦

George Mackay Brown

(1921–96)

I believe that a desert and a seashore and a lake heard for a few years the sweet thrilling music of the Incarnate Word . . . No writer of genius, Dante or Shakespeare or Tolstoy, could have imagined the recorded utterances of Christ . . . there's no story I know of so perfectly shaped and phrased as 'The Prodigal Son' or 'The Good Samaritan' . . . The most awesome and marvellous proof for me is the way he chose to go on nourishing his people after his ascension, in the form of bread. So the brutish life of man is continually possessed, broken, transfigured by the majesty of God.

George Mackay Brown, from *The Tarn and the Rosary*

'George Mackay Brown was a poet, playwright, novelist and an acknowledged master of the short story. This extract is from one of his most autobiographical short stories entitled 'The Tarn and the Rosary'. He lived for most of his life on the Orkney Islands and his writing is immersed in the history and geography of these islands. As an adult he was received into the Roman Catholic Church, and this extract is part of a letter which Colm (his alter-ego) in the story writes to an atheist friend explaining his decision.'

❡ An example of George Mackay Brown's poetry is:

Christmas

'Toll requiem', said sun to earth,
As the grass got thin.
The star-wheel went, all nails and thorns,
Over mill and kirk and inn.

The old sun died. The widowed earth
Tolled a black bell.
'Our King will return,' said root to bone,
To the skeleton tree on the hill.

At midnight, an ox and an ass,
Between lantern and star
Cried, *Gloria . . . Lux in tenebris . . .*
In a wintered byre.

From *Travellers*

The Duke of Wellington
(1769–1852)

My Lord,

If I attempted to answer the mass of futile correspondence which surrounds me, I should be debarred from the serious business of campaigning . . .

So long as I retain an independent position, I shall see no officer under my command is debarred by attending to the futile drivelling of mere quill-driving from attending to his first duty, which is and always has been to train the private men under his command that they may without question beat any force opposed to them in the field.

Duke of Wellington, from a letter written to the
Secretary of State for War during the Peninsular Campaign

'Wellington is a great hero of mine, and this rings a familiar bell: the frustrations of the commander in the field with the bureaucracy of Whitehall.'

THE RT HON. LORD JUSTICE JACOB
Treasurer of Gray's Inn, the Royal Courts of Justice

Richard Feynman
(1918–88)

This freedom to doubt is an important matter in the sciences and, I believe, in other fields. It was born of a struggle to be permitted to doubt, to be unsure . . . I feel a responsibility as a scientist who knows the great value of a satisfactory philosophy of ignorance, and the progress made possible by such a philosophy, progress which is the fruit of freedom of thought. I feel a responsibility to proclaim the value of this freedom and to teach that doubt is not to be feared, but that it is to be welcomed as the possibility of a new potential for human beings. If you know that you are not sure, you have a chance to improve the situation. I want to demand this freedom for future generations.

Richard Feynman, from *The Meaning of it All.*

'Nobel Prize-winning physicist Richard Feynman to me represents rationalism – a major force for good in this increasingly irrational and fundamentalist world.'

DEREK JACOBI

Actor

William Shakespeare

(1564–1616)

What a piece of work is man! how noble in reason! how infinite in faculty! in form and moving how express and admirable! in action how like an angel! in apprehension how like a god! the beauty of the world! the paragon of animals!

William Shakespeare, *Hamlet*, Act II, Scene 2

'My hero has to be Shakespeare, and who has ever said this better?'

P. D. JAMES

Novelist

William Tyndale

(1494–1536)

If God spare my life, ere many years I will cause a boy that driveth the plough shall know more of the Scripture than thou dost.

William Tyndale, spoken by Tyndale to a learned divine before he left England

'One of my favourite heroes is William Tyndale, to whom more than any other single man, we owe our English Bible, a book of such truth, power and beauty that it has become the great glory of Christendom. Tyndale, who was born in 1495, was one of the most remarkable of the Reformation leaders. He was forced to flee England but in 1535 was betrayed, imprisoned at Vilvorde near Brussels, and after 16 months of interrogation, was burned at the stake. But his legacy is imperishable. He is one of the great geniuses of the English language, translating the original Hebrew and Greek into English prose that could be understood by the herdsman in the fields, the weaver at his loom, the cottager and his wife at their fireside. This was his achievement and it is one we should still honour.'

MARTIN JENKINS

Former Chief Producer (Drama) BBC

Kitty Wilkinson

(1786–1860)

Saint of the slums.

Epithet given to Kitty Wilkinson by the people of Liverpool

'In the year in which Liverpool celebrates its status as Capital of Culture, I have chosen Kitty Wilkinson who is commemorated by a stained-glass window in Liverpool's Anglican Cathedral. Although poor herself, she worked tirelessly for the destitute trapped in the city's appalling slums, and her endeavours led to the opening of the world's first public wash-house. She started a children's night-school; sold horse manure; worked in a nail factory; adopted three children irrespective of their religious background; sent food and clothing to the workhouse; distributed Bibles; and, most importantly during the cholera epidemic of 1832, opened her home to all and boiled and washed her neighbours' fever-tainted clothing. Today, her selfless devotion to the care of the sick has been fully recognized.'

TOBY LOVE

Age 11, North Cadbury Church of England Primary School, Somerset

Granny Pop

Granny Pop, she is so cool,
Every day she takes me to school.

Granny Pop, I like her so much,
She really is the big soft touch.

Granny Pop, she tells us funny stories,
Although she has a lot of allergies.

Granny Pop, I love her so,
She's really cool, she goes with the flow.

Granny Pop, she is the best,
She is sometimes overdressed.

Granny Pop, she is herself,
She is better than the sun itself.

Toby Love

REBECCA JOHN

Artist, grand-daughter of Augustus John

Alfred Brendel

(1931–)

For Beethoven, form is the triumph of order over chaos . . . Schubert's forms are a matter of propriety, a 'veil of order' . . . which barely conceals the most beautiful chaos music has ever seen.

Alfred Brendel

'A radio had been left on in the kitchen. I walked in and was electrified by what I heard: Mozart's piano music played with such dazzling vitality and *joie de vivre* that I felt life would change for ever. The pianist was Alfred Brendel. I have never forgotten this moment – nearly 40 years ago now – and have revered Brendel's piano playing ever since. There is the bonus, too, of his writings which offer such insights as his comparison of Beethoven 'the architect', to Schubert 'the sleepwalker', and could be applied to all creative endeavour.'

LETTY JOHNSON

Age 6

Daddy
(1962–)

'Because he helps me and he loves me.'

HUGH JOHNSON

Author of books on wine and trees

Samuel Johnson
(1709–84)

Angling . . . I can only compare to a stick and a string, with a worm at one end and a fool at the other.

Samuel Johnson

'Samuel Johnson has been my hero since I was a boy. In my mind he stands for the sort of no-nonsense Englishness that has never been as common as we would like to think. He had no advantage in life but well-founded self-respect; a sort of jaw-jutting 'Here I stand' that we now think of as Churchillian.

Johnson was a hack (we would say a freelance) earning his living by his pen. Given his unbuyable independence of mind it was hard graft. He was best known in his lifetime for his *Dictionary*, the first of the English language; though better now for Boswell's record of his conversation and behaviour. He wrote literary criticism, an important edition of Shakespeare, *The Lives of the Poets*, a novel, poetry and much else besides (including prayers that bring the language of the Prayer Book into the classical age).

Above all though, he talked. His voice still booms out in the full and sonorous tones of our language, spending his evening at the Turks' Head in Gerrard Street in the company of such fine friends as Edmund Burke, Sir Joshua Reynolds, Oliver Goldsmith, Sheridan, Garrick, Charles James Fox and James Boswell. We can still hear his aphorisms and sound advice, such as "Patriotism is the last refuge of a scoundrel", and "Clear your mind of cant. You may talk in this manner, because it is a mode of talking in society, but don't think foolishly".'

SIR JOHN JOHNSON

Diplomat, conservationist and walker,
former Chairman of the Countryside Commission

Dr David Livingstone

(1813–73)

I have waited years for letters and I have been taught patience. I can surely wait a few hours longer. Now tell me the general news; how is the world getting along?

Dr David Livingstone

'Everyone knows Henry M. Stanley's greeting to the African explorer David Livingstone, but few know this response of Livingstone's, given by him when Stanley, following the initial courtesies, presented him with a bundle of letters. That was in 1871 at Ujiji near Lake Tanganyika. Livingstone loved Africa and its people. He preferred Africans to Europeans as travel companions and is remembered fondly in Africa. His grave, after his seven years of wanderings, is marked by a stone obelisk in savannah woodland deep in what is now Zambia. An elderly African proudly led me to the clearing and said with reverence, "He was a great African".'

DR LUCY JOHNSON

Geriatrician

Sir William Osler

(1849–1919)

. . . An art which consists largely of balancing probabilities.

William Osler, from *The Principles and Practice of Medicine*

'Canadian-born physician William Osler was a humane doctor and teacher: humorous, kind and simultaneously calm and energetic. He was a superb diagnostician, emphasizing the twin keys of listening to the patient's own story and performing a careful examination. He combined an insight into the earthy side of human life with an understanding of the importance of culture, and recommended to his students a tolerant attitude to humans: "The more closely we study their little foibles of one sort or another in the inner life we see, the more surely is the conviction borne upon us of the likeness of their weaknesses to our own. The similarity would be intolerable, if a happy egotism did not often render us forgetful of it."

He accepted uncertainty and encouraged what is now called "reflective learning", suggesting that the doctor should gain wisdom through experience by dividing his diagnoses into "clear cases, doubtful cases and mistakes". I love this description of medicine by him since, every day, I weigh up the risks and benefits of investigations and treatment for individual patients.'

❡ William Osler was also chosen by HARVEY WHITE, surgeon.

THE REVD NOËL JONES
Bishop

Alexander Pope
(1688–1744)

To err is human, to forgive, divine.

Alexander Pope

'I have always admired Pope for his down-to-earth comments and almost "household" truisms. If sometimes cynical, at least he reminds us that our current thinking that humankind can achieve everything, is doomed without reference to the Divine.'

ANNE KARPF
Writer and journalist

Natalia Karp
(1911–2007)

. . . my foreman, a horrible German with a big moustache, came to me and asked in German, 'What have you done?' I said, 'I mopped and the mop fell into the machine.' But I was so furious and so hungry that I was really cheeky. I said to him, 'How long have you been working at this machine?' He said, 'For 25 years.' I said, 'And I have been playing the piano for 25 years. If you play after a fortnight like me, then I'll work after a fortnight like you do.' . . . The following day he brought me a small bottle of red salt . . . And he never behaved to me rudely any more.

Anne Karpf, from The War After: Living with the Holocaust

'This is taken from an interview with my mother, Natalia Karp, a Polish–Jewish concert pianist and survivor of Auschwitz and Płaszów camps (where her piano playing saved her life). She is describing an incident in 1945 in the third and last camp she was in, Lichtewerden. She had to mop the weaving machine she was working on, but hurt herself trying to retrieve her mop which had fallen in.'

¶ Natalia, who had been a soloist with the Berlin Philharmonic at the age of 18, dropped the 'f' of Karpf as her professional name when she resumed her piano career in Britain after the war, but the name on her gravestone which she shares with her husband reads 'Karpf'.

BRIGID KEENAN

Writer

〜 ✍

Rosa Parks

(1913–2005)

She sat down in order that we might stand up.

The Revd Jesse Jackson (1941–), obituary in The New York Times, 2005

'My heroine is Rosa Parks, a black seamstress in Alabama, USA, who in 1955 refused to give up her seat on the bus to a white man. Rosa Parks knew she would be prosecuted, and that she risked physical assault, but she had the courage to sit it out. This defiance by a "nobody" against the cruel and humiliating segregation laws of the time captivated the nation and (though she could not have foreseen this) her action triggered the civil rights movement in the USA. I admire her because her action, and its consequences, show that the most alone and insignificant of us can stand up and make a difference – if we only have the courage.'

¶ Brigid Keenan is married to the European Commission Special Envoy to Azerbaijan, Alan Waddams.

SAM KILEY

Journalist and broadcaster

Pliny the Elder

(AD 23–79)

Ex Africa semper aliquid novi. (There is always something new out of Africa.)

Pliny the Elder

'I don't know much about Pliny, but he was right about Africa.'

MARY KILLEN

Spectator columnist and problem-solver

Archbishop William Temple

(1881–1944)

The Church is the only society that exists for the benefit of those who are not its members.

William Temple

'I've chosen William Temple partly through self-flattery as we are related, in that he was a cousin of my grandmother's. He was said to be the most brilliant Archbishop of Canterbury since Anselm in the eleventh to twelfth century. He held the office from 1942 to 1944. No doubt he was not susceptible to flattery himself.'

¶ William Temple was the son of Archbishop Frederick Temple. It is said that when he was very young he was asked what he wanted to be when he grew up and the grave reply was that he wasn't quite sure if he would prefer to be Archbishop or Prime Minister. He had, it later proved, the academic prowess and social conscience that would have suited him for both roles, but the Church won the day. A theologian with a towering intellect, he also had a reflective depth and simple holiness which engendered great love, both nationally and internationally. His strong belief in the incarnation of Christ inspired him to give outspoken priority to the poor, to instigate lasting programmes of social and Church reforms and to lay foundations for Church unity – all against the background of a society that was still bound by class and racial and sexual prejudice. He famously said, 'When God supervenes we do not find a human being taken into fellowship with God but God acting through the conditions supplied by humanity.' He was also blessed with a quick sense of humour and of the ridiculous. One story tells of him greeting an official visitor with, 'Please take a seat Mr Smith.' The icy response was, 'My name, Sir, is Fordingbrass-Smith.' To which his warm reply was, 'Oh dear, I'm so sorry, please do take two seats.'

TIM KIRKBRIDE

Retired company director

Andrew Marvell

(1621–78)

From *An Horation Ode Upon Cromwell's Return from Ireland*

> On King Charles I:
> He nothing common did or mean
> Upon that memorable scene,
> But with his keener eye
> The axe's edge did try;
>
> Nor called the Gods, with vulgar spite,
> To vindicate his helpless right;
> But bow'd his comely head
> Down, as upon a bed.

'I admire Andrew Marvell both as a poet and diplomat. He was obliged to eulogize Cromwell but these two verses show a feeling for Charles.'

❡ Charles I said on the scaffold on 30 January 1649: 'And therefore I tell you (and I pray God it be not laid to your charge) that I am the Martyr of the People.'

Prince Rupert

(1619–82)

I must extremely lament their condition, being exposed to all ruin and slavery. One comfort will be left: we shall all fall together. When this is, remember I have done my duty. Your faithful Friend, Rupert.

Prince Rupert, from a letter to the Duke of Richmond, 28 July 1645

'This is Prince Rupert aged 25, worn down after three years of non-stop campaigning for a king who was forever changing his mind, on the fate of the King's few remaining supporters following the catastrophic defeat at Naseby.

Although I do not have personal heroes, Prince Rupert is definitely heroic. As a commander by land and sea, Prince Rupert earned undying fame for his outstanding bravery in battle, but there is more to it than that. He was grandson of one king of England, nephew of another and first cousin to a third. He was commander-in-chief of the king's army in the Civil War and later of his son's fleet, first against the Commonwealth and then against the Dutch. He was a conscientious member of the Privy Council in both reigns and during much of the interregnum. He was influential in laying the foundations of empire in Africa and Canada and was respected as a scientist and as an artist. As a commander of land forces his achievements did not last because they were swallowed up in the wreck of the Royalist cause. As an admiral and as a director of England's naval affairs, he played an important part in preparing the Royal Navy for its supremacy at sea, which lasted for two-and-a-half centuries.

Rupert was immensely tall, handsome and athletic. He was renowned for his violent temper but also for a degree of honesty and integrity, rarely found among men of power during the seventeenth century. He did not marry, but was never short of female company. He sired a son who was killed fighting the Turks, and a daughter whose descendants are still around. He continues to attract interest and new biographies appear with great regularity.'

SIR ROBIN KNOX-JOHNSTON
Master mariner

John Davis
(1550–1605)

Oh Lord, if we are to die, I would rather it were to be in advancing than in retreating.

John Davis

'I admire Davis enormously. He was one of the greatest sailors and pilots of his day. He sought the North Passage through the Arctic (hence the Davis Straits), and piloted Dutch and English expeditions to the East Indies. He accompanied, among others, Raleigh and Cavendish. The latter was a less savoury character and freebooter who, with Davis, completed the third navigation of the world after Magellan and Drake. Their passage through the narrow Magellan Straits in their cumbersome boats tacking against the wind was a tremendous feat. I chose the "easier" route around Cape Horn. At least there was more sea room to navigate through the difficult seas.'

¶ Davis invented a backstaff and a double quadrant still in use 200 years after his death. He also made his own attempt on the Magellan Straits and discovered the Falkland Islands. Having defied the oceans he was killed by Japanese pirates off Bintang, near Sumatra.

Robin Knox-Johnston completed his third solo circumnavigation of the world on 4 May 2007. The treacherous waves around Cape Horn can reach heights of over 60 feet, sometimes staggeringly sheer and with the full force of the Pacific behind them.

JETJE KRAEMER
Retired teacher and Project Officer for ICCO*

Frits Eisenloeffel
(1944–2001)

'I am not a hero-worshipper. But I am inspired and get warmed up by people who love life, have humour, stand up for justice and show in practice what solidarity means and accept what comes to them. In my eyes, my friend and colleague Frits Eisenloeffel was such a person.'

❡ Frits Eisenloeffel, photographer, writer and TV film-maker, covered liberation struggles and wars in Africa and undertook several missions to Sudan and Eritrea in support of the Eritrean liberation struggle. On his last journey in 1985 he was struck down by a stroke. He fought for recovery against all odds, but died of another stroke in 2001.

*ICCO works worldwide to help eliminate poverty and injustice. Its roots are in the Dutch Protestant Churches but it co-operates with any organization that shares its ideals.

PROFESSOR BENJAMIN LAMBERTON

Attorney and Professorial Lecturer in Law, Washington

Shaikh Ahmad al-'Alawī (1869–1934)

Faith is necessary for religions, but it ceases to be so for those who go further and who achieve self-realization in God. Then one no longer believes because one sees. There is no longer any need to believe, when one *sees* the Truth.

Shaikh Ahmad al-'Alawī, Sufi wise man, said to his friend Dr Marcel Carret.
From A *Moslem Saint of the Twentieth Century*, by Martin Lings

'This fascinating concept is not limited to the Islamic tradition of Sufism. It is also to be found in the Gospel of Thomas and other Gnostic texts. It opens the door to a different path towards God.'

❡ Shaikh Ahmad al-'Alawī was a popular Sufi mystic and ascetic. His centre, the Zāwiyah (nook) was in Tigitt, Algeria, and his lifestyle was reminiscent of the early Christian Desert Fathers. The essence of his teaching was based on the opening of oneself to the direct experience of God.

W. B. Yeats

(1865–1939)

Myself must I remake.

W. B. Yeats, from *An Acre of Grass*

'I love this quote almost more out of context.'

¶ The whole verse is as follows:

> Grant me an old man's frenzy,
> Myself must I remake
> Till I am Timon and Lear
> Or that William Blake
> Who beat upon the wall
> Till Truth obeyed his call.

ADMIRAL SIR MICHAEL LAYARD

Alfred the Great

(*c.* 848–99)

The king set up great schools where the sons of nobles and rich freeman might learn Latin, English, horsemanship and falconry. He likewise commanded the preparation of an Anglo-Saxon Chronicle, which should record the chief happenings of each year and is so valuable to us today.

Andre Maurois, from *A History of England*

'Alfred the Great is my hero because in the darkest days of the Dark Ages he was a beacon of courage, leadership and learning. He led his Anglo-Saxon people to withstand and eventually defeat the pagan invaders and kept Wessex English while the rest of the country succumbed. He formed the first standing army and was the founder of the Royal Navy. With astounding intellect and foresight he transformed the function of law and learning and led his poor, illiterate people into an educated, Christian and well-ordered society that was a blueprint for the future. He was a hero – "Great" indeed.'

¶ Alfred is the only English monarch to whom the appellation 'Great' is given.

HUGH LEACH

Retired soldier and diplomat

Mu'awiyah Ibn Abu Sufyan

(d. 680), sixth Islamic Caliph, Governor of Syria and founder of the Umayyad dynasty

I apply not my sword where my lash suffices, nor my lash where my tongue is enough. And even if there be but one hair binding me to my fellow men, I do not let it break. When they pull, I loosen; and if they loosen, I pull.

Mu'awiyah Ibn Abu Sufyan

'Known as the "Arab Caesar", Mu'awiyah was one of the most successful generals during the early Arab conquests. Courteous and patient, and a near-genius, he recognized that war was a last resort in any dispute. He understood that the former leaders of the newly conquered territories and those early Arab soldiers had first to be consulted, then persuaded, before they could be commanded successfully. This dictum has often been quoted by successive Arab administrations, and is well understood, even today, by anyone who has worked with highly independent Arab irregulars.'

Charles-Maurice de Talleyrand-Périgord

(1754–1838), French statesman, diplomat and priest

Human life is like a game of chess – each piece holds its place upon the chessboard – King, Queen, Bishop and Pawn. Death comes, the game is up, and all are thrown, without distinction, pell-mell in the same bag.

Charles-Maurice de Talleyrand

'There have been many sayings about how the good and the great and the unknown are all equal in death. This by Talleyrand with its allusion to a common game is, I think, one of the best.'

JOHN LEACH

Third-generation potter

Mahatma Gandhi

(1869–1948)

I think it would be a good idea.

> Gandhi's reply when asked what he thought of western civilization

'I think Gandhi's words highlight the post-colonial attitudes that still exist in the west. Why, for instance, do we use the term 'Third World', as if it were a world that should be put in its place?'

❡ This episode may have occurred when Gandhi visited Lancashire some time before India was granted independence. He asked the cotton manufacturers to remember that India grew and manufactured its own cotton and to think carefully before exporting cotton goods to India.

ALICE LEAHY

Director and co-founder of TRUST;
Member of the Irish Human Rights Commission

Professor James McCormick

(1926–2007)

The Nature of Homelessness
People who are homeless have often rejected the conventional values of society or have been themselves rejected. It is not surprising that many have been in prison or mental hospitals or both. In a society which is intolerant, imprisonment or admission to a mental hospital is the usual response. In the view of most people, these

'unfortunates' are failures; failures who are largely to blame for their own misfortunes, failures whose very existence is an embarrassment and shame.

The reality is, of course, different. Once set on a downward path such people may readily enter a spiral which ensures that they have less and less in common with those who have loving families, houses and regular income. They have little reason to trust others, little to look forward to and little to remember with pleasure.

Professor James McCormick

'Professor James McCormick, writer, lecturer and retired doctor, was Head of the Department of Community Health in Trinity College Dublin, and Chairman of TRUST. Wise, inspiring and generous, he was committed to the outsiders in our society and restoring their dignity; and challenged us to question the world we live in and the nature of exclusion.'

❡ The TRUST charity provides medical and related services for homeless people, and is involved in prison and psychiatric work.

ANDREA SENE

Age 11, Lorretto Convent Junior School, Gibraltar

St Bernadette

(1844–1879)

Bernadette saw the lady every day,
Every time she saw her they said a Rosary
Really Bernadette saw her eighteen times,
Nobody believed her.
And she wore a white and blue dress,
Died at the age of thirty-six,
Everyone soon believed her,
Today the Virgin Mary has great following,
Time went past, day by day,
Eighteen times she went to see her.

Andrea Sene

THE HON. JOHN BARNABAS LEITH

Principal Representative, Diplomatic Relations,
for the Bahá'í community of the UK

~~ ~~

Abdu'l-Bahá

(1844–1921)

The Blessed Beauty saith: 'Ye are all the fruits of one tree, the leaves of one branch.' Thus has He likened this world of being to a single tree, and all its peoples to the leaves thereof, and the blossoms and fruits. It is needful for the bough to blossom, and the leaf and fruit to flourish, and upon the interconnection of all parts of the world-tree, dependeth the flourishing of leaf and blossom, and the sweetness of the fruit.

For this reason must all human beings powerfully sustain one another and seek for everlasting life . . . Let them at all times concern themselves with doing a kindly thing for one of their fellows, offering to someone love, consideration, thoughtful help. Let them see no-one as their enemy, or as wishing them ill, but think of all humankind as their friends; regarding the alien as an intimate, the stranger as a companion, staying free of prejudice, drawing no lines.

From The Writings of Abdu'l-Bahá

'My hero is a spiritual giant, Abdu'l-Bahá. He was the eldest son of Bahá'u'lláh, the prophet-founder of the Bahá'í faith. Abdu'l-Bahá shared his father's imprisonments, exiles and privations and showed extraordinary spiritual and practical wisdom from an early age.

When he succeeded his father in 1892 as head of the Bahá'í community, he took the title 'Abdu'l-Bahá, and thus stressed the importance of service in his life and the life of all Bahá'ís. From his continuing confinement in Acre in Palestine by the Ottomans, Abdu'l-Bahá maintained a voluminous correspondence with the Bahá'ís worldwide. His burial place on the slopes of Mount Carmel is a place of pilgrimage for Bahá'ís all over the world.'

Retired orthodontist and now Patron of the
Northern Ireland Council for Integrated Education

Gerard Manley Hopkins

(1844–89)

God's Grandeur

The world is charged with the grandeur of God.
It will flame out, like shining from shook foil;
It gathers to a greatness, like the ooze of oil
Crushed. Why do men then now not reck his rod?
Generations have trod, have trod, have trod;
And all is seared with trade; bleared, smeared with toil;
And wears man's smudge and shares man's smell: the soil
Is bare now, nor can foot feel, being shod.
And for all this, nature is never spent;
There lives the dearest freshness deep down things;
And though the last lights off the black West went
Oh, morning, at the brown brink eastward, springs –
Because the Holy Ghost over the bent
World broods with warm breast and with ah! Bright wings.

Gerard Manley Hopkins

'Manley Hopkins is not just a poet – he is a composer with words. Read
him out loud and you will hear the beauty of nature.'

¶ Cecil Linehan is co-founder of All Children Together, a movement founded
in the early 1970s for the advancement of integrated schools for Catholic and
Protestant children in Northern Ireland. At that time, segregation in education
along religious lines was almost 100 per cent. There are now 62 integrated
schools right across Northern Ireland catering for over 18,000 pupils aged from
four to eighteen.

JULIAN LITCHFIELD

Innkeeper, The Halfway House

Gilbert White

(1720–93)

Gilbert White discovered this formula for complete happiness, but he died before making the announcement. It is, to be very busy with the unimportant.

A. Edward Newton (1863–1940), from *This Book Collecting Game*

❡ Gilbert White wrote his *Natural History of Selborne*, which is in the form of letters to two friends, over a period of about 14 years and it was finally published another 14 years later in 1789. An extract from letter XL is: 'The flycatcher is of all our summer birds the most mute and the most familiar; it also appears the last of any. It builds in a vine, or a sweetbriar, against the wall of an house, or in the hole of a wall, or on the end of a beam or plate, and often close to the post of a door where people are going in and out all day long. This bird does not make the least pretension to song, but uses a little inward wailing note when it thinks its young in danger from cats or other annoyances: it breeds but once, and retires early.'

THE REVD SISTER HELEN LODER

Priest and leader of St Saviour's Priory Community

Monica Furlong

(1930–2003)

A Reassessment

St Monica
Is not my favourite saint.
Moral blackmail
Is not an attractive taint.

'Give up your mistress,' she said
And your little son, Adeodatus
Or I'll cry, Augustine, I'll cry,
Mummy *will* be grieved;
(not to mention God);
And she was, Augustine, she was.

Poor Augustine,
No wonder he harped so
On original sin
Gave up his delicious affair
And took to chastity in despair.

Monica Furlong, from *Prayers and Poems*

'Monica Furlong, Christian intellectual and mystic, writer, feminist and campaigner, was a witty and irreverent thorn in the flesh of the Anglican Church. Fearless in the pursuit of truth, she campaigned in the 1970s for the acceptance of gay clergy and later for the ordination of women. My gratitude for her energy and inspiration is boundless.'

JOHN LONERGAN

Governor, Mountjoy Prison, Dublin

Edmund Burke

(1729–97)

If we command our wealth, we shall be rich and free. If our wealth commands us, we shall be poor indeed.

Edmund Burke

'Edmund Burke lived over 200 years ago when Ireland was a poor country. Today, Ireland is regarded as one of the most affluent countries in Europe. However, Burke's philosophy is more relevant today. During the eighteenth century he was a prophet and a visionary.'

Sir Bernard Lovell

Founder, Jodrell Bank Observatory

Alfred North Whitehead

(1861–1947)

Apart from the intervention of God there could be nothing new in the world, and no order in the world.

Alfred North Whitehead, from *Process and Reality*

'As a young student I was greatly impressed by Alfred North Whitehead, the great philosopher and mathematician, particularly in his efforts to develop the metaphysical system bringing aesthetic, moral and religious concepts into relation with natural science.'

Brigadier Peter Lyddon

Retired army officer and Canon Emeritus of York Minster

Nelson Mandela

(1918–)

Today, all of us, by our presence here . . . confer glory and hope to newborn liberty. Out of the experience of an extraordinary human disaster that lasted too long, must be born a society of which all humanity will be proud.

Never, never, and never again shall it be that this beautiful land will again experience the oppression of one by another . . . The sun shall never set on so glorious a human achievement. Let freedom reign. God bless Africa!

Nelson Mandela, from his presidential inaugural speech, 10 May 1994

(quoted in his book *Long Walk to Freedom*)

'He is an amazing human being. Incarcerated for 27 years, of which 18 years were spent in solitary confinement in a cell on Robben Island, and yet he still maintained his dignity and trust in his fellow man. Need I say more?'

Richard Mabey
Writer, naturalist

Non-Heroes

What the world needs – and always needed – is plenty of determined *ordinary* people.

Richard Mabey, 6 September 2007

Claire Macdonald
Cook and author

Lucrezia Borgia
(1480–1519)

'Lucrezia Borgia is notorious by her name, and much maligned for that reason. Becoming Lucrezia D'Este after her third marriage, she did immeasurable good in Ferrara, then the home base of the D'Este family. She became a deeply devout and selfless woman, suffering a great deal physically. She was a stoic and deserves far more recognition than she is usually afforded. Her father and brother were truly evil, yet Lucrezia was anything but.'

¶ Lucrezia's second husband Alfonso of Aragon was assassinated, most probably by her brother Cesare Borgia, the one-time Cardinal and son, by his mistress Vannozza dei Catanei, of Rodrigo Borgia, later Pope Alexander VI. Never had the Church been more dishonoured, worldly and corrupt than under the Borgias. Bent on a policy of self-aggrandizement and the acquisition of land

and titles, they used perfidy, treachery and murder to gain their aspirations. They funded their large army which pillaged at will, by seizing the property of their victims and selling church offices. Cesare was extolled by Machiavelle in *Il Principe*, leaving us the dubious adage, 'The end justifies the means'.

Stuart MacFarlane
Builder

Robert Burns
(1759–96)

Who ere you are
Where ere you be
Let your wind go free.
Robert Burns

'Burns, as well as being brilliant, is a down-to-earth poet for everyone.'

Michael MacKay-Lewis
Engineer

Thich Nhat Hanh
(b. 1926)

There is no way to happiness – happiness is the way.
Thich Nhat Hanh

'Thich Nhat Hanh, a Vietnamese Zen Buddhist Monk, was a peace activist during the Vietnamese war and has now set up Plum Village in south-west France – a meditation and retreat centre for all ages.'

SIR DONALD MAITLAND

Former diplomat

Sir Winston Churchill

(1874–1965)

Talking jaw-jaw is always better than war-war.
Winston Churchill, from a speech in the White House, Washington, 26 June 1954

DAME ELIZA MANNINGHAM-BULLER

Former Director General of the Security Service (MI5)

St Paul

(d. c. 65 CE)

Whatsoever things are true, whatsoever things are honest, whatsoever things are just, whatsoever things are pure, whatsoever things are lovely, whatsoever things are of good report; if there be any virtue and if there be any praise, think on these things.

Philippians 4.8 (AV)

'I have chosen this quote as it reminds me of my mother.'

CAPTAIN MICHAEL MANSERGH RN

Commanding Officer of HMS *Ark Royal*

William Blake

(1757–1827)

Bring me my bow of burning gold!
Bring me my arrows of desire!
Bring me my spear! O clouds, unfold!
Bring me my chariot of fire!

I will not cease from mental fight
Nor shall my sword sleep in my hand,
Till we have built Jerusalem,
In England's green and pleasant land.

William Blake, from preface to *Milton*

'For me, these lines, immortalized in the hymn by C. H. Parry, are always a positive encouragement in adversity. They symbolize William Blake's vision of the power and determination of mankind to strive for a better world.'

MANDY MARTIN

Australian artist

Janangoo Butcher Cherel

(1920–)

With my eyes, my heart and with my brain I am thinking. When I sleep night-time, I might talk to myself, 'Ah, I might paint that one tomorrow'. Not dreaming, I think about what to do next day.

Janangoo Butcher Cherel

'I'm a great admirer of the work of Butcher Cherel, one of the most prominent and senior painters in the Kimberley. He is now 87 and paints at the art centre at a dedicated table, and his signature iconography of rounded hills and interconnected bone designs is instantly recognizable.

Janangoo Butcher Cherel of the Gooniyandi-Kija people was born in Fossil Downs, an area of about one million acres. He worked there until in his sixties. While painting there recently with him it was intriguing to watch him rotate his canvases and work from all sides. As the day warmed, a small willie-willie blew my canvas off my easel and Butcher broke into traditional song. It was as if he was singing inside his head quite a bit of the day, just as he dreams his paintings when he is awake and asleep.'

❡ Mandy Martin is a leading Australian artist who, among other things, was commissioned to produced a major work, 'Red Ochre Cove', for Parliament House in Canberra in 1988.

Sir Clive Martin

Lord Mayor of London 1999–2000

❦

Colonel Colin Wylie

(1918–2007)

A Schoolboy's Appreciation of his Great-grandfather
My hero is my great-grandfather who was born in India in 1918, where he grew up. He married my great-grandmother, Claudia, in England in 1940. They had known each other in India and at school in Bedford. The war had already begun and he was married in his uniform. He was an engineer called a Sapper. He was captured by the Germans very early on, and spent most of the war in prisoner-of-war camps. He escaped from them all, except Colditz. His sheets went into Airey Neave's famous 'plane – I've seen a model of it in the Imperial War Museum. He didn't meet my grandmother until the war was over. He is a very wise and generous man. He taught my

mother about flowers, birds, butterflies and birdsong. Now he is teaching me.

When he was in Colditz, he painted beautiful paintings that he sent to my great-granny. We also recently found a treasure box of photographs, including some of when he was in Colditz, looking a bit like Brad Pitt! He was a bit of a rebel, and while everyone else seemed to be in uniform, he was wearing a cravat and jumper! I'm so lucky to know my great-grandfather. We write to each other often and he tells me funny stories about his life. I hope I can live my life as well as him.

Harry Nightingale, written in 2006, aged 10

'At the crossroads of life, from time to time we meet someone who points the way to the future. Thus did Major Colin Wylie influence the fledgling subaltern who arrived in BAOR in 1957. Colin was my hero. Like many others he rarely spoke of his wartime experiences and never sought recognition of his military achievements.

Colin's visible contribution to mankind was the profound influence he had on the development of young people, including myself aged 22, his grand-daughters, and his great-grandson Harry.'

Anna Massey

Actress

Confucius

(551–479 BC)

This too shall pass.

Confucius

'This saying has helped me often in my life. When you are passing through difficult times it gives hope, and when you are passing through good times it encourages you to treasure these moments, for they too shall pass!'

Robert Maxwell Wood

Artist/painter

Eugène Delacroix

(1798–1863)

I can paint you the skin of Venus with mud, provided you let me surround it as I will.

Eugène Delacroix

'Zeus commissioned a race of mortals from Prometheus, who, according to legend, went on to fashion the human race from mud and tears. Bidding for immortality, Delacroix, in what would be a triumphant reversal of roles, threatened to recreate the Roman goddess of love using mud, or indeed the colour thereof, in paint and on canvas. At the time when Delacroix is reported to have made this claim, he was the most celebrated painter in France.

I have to admire the supreme gung-ho self-confidence of this man, while also recognizing that it is indeed possible to render a turbid or unpromising colour beautiful by the sensitive selection and modification of the surrounding hues.'

Alexander Mayer-Rieckh

Director, Security System Reform Program,
International Centre for Transitional Justice

Pedro Arrupe

(1907–91)

Take Jesus Christ from my life and everything would collapse – like a human body from which someone removed the skeleton, heart, and head.

Pedro Arrupe, from *One Jesuit's Spiritual Journey. Autobiographical Conversations with Jean-Claude Dietsch. Selected Letters and Addresses*

'Father Pedro Arrupe, a leading Jesuit and native of Bilbao, Spain, was living in suburban Hiroshima when the atomic bomb fell in August 1945. He was later elected the Superior General of the Society of Jesus. A man of deep spirituality combined with openness for the world, he inspired all he met, working long hours and sleeping little. He encouraged the Jesuits to focus on both the service of faith and the promotion of justice.'

❡ This is an edited version of Father Pedro Arrupe's experience after the bomb fell on Hiroshima:

'I was in my room with another priest at 8.15 when suddenly we saw a blinding light, like a flash of magnesium. As I opened the door which faced the city, we heard a formidable explosion similar to the blast of a hurricane. At the same time doors, windows and walls fell upon us in smithereens.

'We climbed a hill to get a better view. From there we could see a ruined city: before us was a decimated Hiroshima. Since it was at a time when the first meal was being prepared in all the kitchens, the flames contacting the electric current turned the entire city into one enormous flake of fire within two and a half hours.

'I shall never forget my first sight of what was the result of the atomic bomb: a group of young women, 18 or 20 years old, clinging to one another as they dragged themselves along the road.

'The following day at five in the morning, I celebrated Mass. In these very moments, one feels more deeply the value of God's aid. The chapel, half destroyed, was overflowing with the wounded, who were lying on the floor very near to one another, suffering terribly, twisted with pain.'

He utilized his medical skills in the service of the wounded and the dying, transforming the novitiate into a makeshift hospital for over 200 grievously scarred human survivors.

DON MCCULLIN

Photographer

Daniel Barenboim

(1942–)

As Daniel Barenboim demonstrated with his West-Eastern Divan Orchestra, when people of differing views are brought together in a collaborative and creative endeavour, differences become subsumed. The give and take of making music for instance, of listening to the articulation of a phrase by one musician so that it can be answered, or echoed, with corresponding inflection by another, is an act of communion that can transcend politics and religion. Indeed it becomes a kind of shared worship at the altar of human imagination and it is surely there that we need to look for real hope.'

Michael Berkeley, composer/broadcaster, quoted in the Guardian

'I respect Barenboim for his talent, energy, idealism and courage in trying to unite Palestinians and Israelis, and his deep-seated faith that music is a universal language which can cut through all manner of boundaries and barriers – geographical and political and otherwise.'

RICHARD MERYON

Retired Captain, Royal Navy

Daniel

(605–535 BC)

The people who know their God shall be strong, and carry out great exploits.

Daniel 11.32b, NKJV

'Daniel, from the age of 15, stood as a Godly man in the alien land of Babylon. He served Nebuchadnezzar, Belshazzar and Darius; and because of his witness and work saw Nebuchadnezzar and Darius acknowledge God.'

¶ Belshazzar, the son of Nebuchadnezzar, king of Babylon, became a tyrant and was overthrown by Darius the Mede. Stories in the book include the escape from the burning fiery furnace, the writing on the wall at Belshazzar's feast and that of Daniel in the lions' den. The book may not, however, have been written by Daniel but at a later date circa 168–165 BC during a period of persecution by the Seleucid Emperor Antiochus Epiphanes.

William James

(1842–1910)

Ninety nine hundredths or possibly nine hundred and ninety nine thousandths of our activity is purely automatic and habitual . . . Education is for behaviour, and habits are the stuff of which our behaviour consists.

William James, from *Talk to Teachers*, 1895

'As a teacher I admired William James' writings and his ideas which helped me a lot.'

❡ William James was the older brother of the novelist Henry James. A philosopher and psychologist, he co-founded the American Society for Psychical Research.

St Monica

(c. 332–87)

Lay this body wherever it may be, let not the care of it disturb you. This only I ask of you, that you should remember me at the altar of the Lord, wherever you may be.

St Monica's dying words to her son St Augustine

'I am fond of St Monica because she reminds me of my mother, especially in that she was constantly concerned about her son St Augustine, particularly when he went "off the rails". When he was finally "back on track" it was a mother's dream fulfilled.'

William Blake

(1757–1827)

To see a world in a grain of sand
And a heaven in a wild flower,
Hold infinity in the palm of your hand
And eternity in an hour.

William Blake, from
Auguries of Innocence, c. 1803

He was energy itself, and shed around him a kindling influence; an atmosphere of life, full of the idea. To walk with him in the country was to perceive the soul of beauty through the forms of matter; and the high gloomy buildings between which, from his stuffy window, a glimpse was caught of the Thames and the Surrey shore, assumed a kind of grandeur from the man dwelling near them ... He was a man without a mask; his aim single, his path straight forwards and his wants few ... If asked whether I ever knew, among the intellectual, a happy man, Blake would be the only one who would immediately occur to me.

Samuel Palmer, painter, in a letter to Blake's first biographer
Alexander Gilchrist, around 1861

'Read his poems. Sing his songs. Drink in his paintings. Wonder at the courage and integrity of his life and that of his wife, Catherine.'

Dr Arthur Mitchell

Retired GP and rebellious conversationalist

Arthur Fowweather

(1901–92)

Would'st be a hero? Wait not then supinely
For deeds of derring-do which no day brings.
The finest life lies oft in doing finely
A multitude of unromantic things.

A. E. Fogg, from the introduction to *Up Down*
by Arthur Fowweather

'Arthur Fowweather was my own Mr Chips and Headmaster at my High School in Downpatrick. In Lancashire, he lived through a grim childhood plagued with ill health. It left him small in stature but with a dogged determination and impressive personality. Because of his chemistry degree, he ended up, in the Second World War, in the Royal Army Ordnance Corps dealing with all things explodable. On his return he imparted the skills of learning to children who had their minds elsewhere. They found that they enjoyed the bizarre such as algebra, trigonometry, science, languages and even poetry. They were imbued not only with knowledge but with the yearning to seek it. Arthur's pupils were his family, whom he influenced in his unique, sensitive yet enthusiastic way. He gave them their futures.'

❡ Perhaps this was the A. E. Fogg from Bolton, who refereed the FA Cup Final match in 1934, and a Northern Ireland versus Scotland match in 1929, but this could not be verified.

NOEL MITCHELL

Honorary Fellow, Queen's University, Belfast

✵ ✵

Ernest Shackleton

(1874–1922)

For scientific leadership give me Scott, for swift and efficient travel, Amundsen. But when you are in a hopeless situation, when you are seeing no way out, get down on your knees and pray for Shackleton. Incomparable in adversity, he was the miracle worker who could save your life against all the odds and long after your number was up. The greatest leader that ever came on God's earth, bar none.

Sir Raymond Priestly (1886–1974)

'I have interest in both polar regions, thanks to my old professor at Glasgow University, who had been Shackleton's scientific adviser on the Ross Sea party. I spent time with the New Zealanders at Scott Base a long time ago, but every day is still well remembered. Shackleton and Crean, his companion, are at last accepted in Eire as heroes, and Shackleton now appears on an Eire stamp.'

❡ Raymond Priestly accompanied Shackleton on the Arctic Nimrod expedition, 1907–9, and Scott's South Polar expedition, 1910–13. The editor met Shackleton's nephew in the 1970s. He told her of that impossible walk, which Shackleton and five others achieved, frozen, starving and exhausted across the unmapped mountainous island of South Georgia, following an 800-mile journey in an open whale boat. He told how Shackleton and his companions were convinced that, throughout, a seventh person walked with them.

SIR DAVID MONEY-COUTTS

Banker

St John the Evangelist

(First century)

For God so loved the world that he gave his one and only Son, that whoever believes in him shall not perish but have eternal life. For God did not send his Son into the world to condemn the world, but to save the world through him.

John 3.16–17 (NIV)

'St John was inspired by his hero, Jesus, the greatest hero of all time, to write this passage which encapsulates the Christian faith. At a time when Christians were often persecuted, he did not hesitate to write up, in his Gospel, all Jesus' teachings and, in the book of Revelation, to publish the prophecy of the end times as revealed to him on the island of Patmos. His writings are as relevant today as they were in the first century AD.'

❡ St John the Evangelist, known as St John the Divine, was also chosen by FRANK WILLIAMS, actor, who played the vicar in *Dad's Army*.

WILLIAM MONTGOMERY

Director of Sotheby's

'One of the Chiefs of Cuba'

Whether you are divinities or mortal men we know not. You have come into these countries with a force against which we were inclined to resist; resistance would be folly: we are all therefore at your mercy. But if you are men subject to mortality like ourselves you cannot be unapprised that after this life there is another, wherein a very different portion is allotted to good and bad men. If

---

therefore you expect to die and believe with us that everyone is rewarded in a future state according to his conduct in the present, you will do no hurt to those who do no hurt to you.

One of the Chiefs of Cuba, in a speech of welcome to Christopher Columbus

'I use this passage a lot when talking, it is one of my favourite quotations; however, little is known about its source. I found it in a favourite anthology of mine, *Love is my Meaning* by Elizabeth Basset, who was lady-in-waiting to the Queen Mother.'

BRIDGET MORETON

Artist

St Molaise

(d. 570)

'St Patrick, who brought Christianity to Ireland, had been dead for a hundred years when St Molaise founded his monastery on the low-lying island of Devenish in beautiful Lough Erne. The high, round spike of its tower still stands there. My parents lived within sight of the tower, so St Molaise (pronounced *Mollasha*) was someone I have known about all my conscious life. I particularly love knowing that when he heard a bird sing he became lost in wonder and adoration, recognizing in it the voice of the Holy Spirit. Lough Erne is full of an orchestra of birdsong threaded with the haunting cry of curlews and the croaks and alarms of waterfowl. I think of St Molaise often, wherever I am in the world.'

¶ St Molaise was born in Ireland, brought up in Scotland and lived on Holy Island as a hermit. He later returned to Ireland where he continued his ministry.

THE RT REVD VAUGHAN MORGAN

Former Principal Roman Catholic Chaplain (Navy),
parish priest in Charlbury

Father James Wamser

(1910?–85?)

I bend the bow as much as I can, not to break it but to make it shoot a little further.

Father James Wamser

'Father James Wamser SJ was the rector at my residential college attached to Innsbruck University. A Jesuit, he was in charge of our daily life and priestly formation. A man of total dedication, he tempered the necessary firm guidance with kindness.'

JAN MORRIS

Author

Sir Edmund Hillary

(1919–2008)

Well George, we've knocked the bastard off!

Sir Edmund Hillary, following the first ascent of Everest in 1953

'I greatly admired the dear old boy, whom I knew for more than 50 years, because he was brave and tough, never lost his native simplicity, and spent his later years helping the Sherpas of the Everest region, the very people who had helped him to his fame.'

¶ Jan Morris accompanied the 1953 Everest expedition as a journalist with *The Times*, reaching a height of some 22,000 feet (though she says that in retrospect it gets higher every year). It was a famous race to get the news back in time for the Coronation on 2 June.

LADY MORSE
Author and former London Tourist Guide

George Herbert
(1593–1633)

Love

Love bade me welcome; yet my soul drew back,
Guilty of dust and sin.
But quick-eyed Love, observing me grow slack
From my first entrance in,
Drew nearer to me, sweetly questioning
If I lacked anything.

'A guest,' I answered, 'worthy to be here':
Love said, 'You shall be he.'
'I, the unkind, ungrateful? Ah my dear!,
I cannot look on Thee.'
Love took my hand, and smiling did reply,
'Who made the eyes but I?'

'Truth Lord, but I have marred them: let my shame
Go where it deserve.'
'And know you not,' says Love, 'who bore the blame?'
'My dear, then I will serve.'
'You must sit down,' says Love, 'and taste my meat.'
So I did sit and eat.

George Herbert, the final poem from *The Temple*

'Herbert's little church, St Andrew's at Bemerton, lies just outside the gates of Wilton, home of his kinsman, the Earl of Pembroke. His rectory, opposite, had gardens which stretched down to the river Nadder, and twice weekly he walked across the water meadows to Evensong at Salisbury Cathedral. It is said that at his induction, Herbert (as was the custom) was locked into the church to ring the bells. He did not emerge, and instead was found kneeling at the altar praying.

This poem indicates how out of sympathy Herbert was with the Puritans: he and his great friend Nicholas Ferrar of Little Gidding were on the side of Laud, and liked to think of the Church "adorned as a bride for her husband".

When I worked as a tourist guide I had the pleasure of taking a group to both Bemerton and Wilton, and found it an inspiring experience.'

¶ Herbert gave up the high life of court and academia to serve as a country parson. *The Temple* was published after his death at the early age of 39.

George Herbert was also chosen by RUSSELL TWISK and WILLIAM REID.

SIR JEREMY MORSE
Retired banker

St Augustine of Hippo
(354–430)

So I was speaking, and weeping in the most bitter contrition of my heart, when lo! I heard from a neighbouring house a voice, as of boy or girl, I know not, chanting and oft repeating, 'Take up and read; Take up and read'. Instantly my countenance altered, I began to think most intently, whether children were wont in any kind of play to sing such words: nor could I remember ever to have heard the like. So checking the torrent of my tears, I arose; interpreting it to be no other than a command from God to open the book and read the first chapter I should find . . . Eagerly then I returned to the place where Alypius was sitting; for there had I laid the volume of the Apostle, when I arose thence. I seized, opened, and in silence read the section on which my eyes first fell: 'Not in rioting and drunkenness, not in chambering and wantonness, not in strife and envying: but put ye on the Lord Jesus Christ, and make not provision for the flesh' in concupiscence. No further would I read; nor needed I: for instantly at the end of this sentence, by a light as it were of serenity, infused into my heart, all the darkness of doubt vanished away.

St Augustine, from *The Confessions of St Augustine*, Book VIII, XII, 29

'*The Confessions of St Augustine* is the first autobiography memorable for the depth of its self-analysis. Among many moving passages, I have chosen the famous account of his final conversion in the garden of his Milan home in 386 AD'.

SIR JOHN MORTIMER

Barrister, playwright and author

Lord Byron

(1788–1824)

When one subtracts from life infancy (which is vegetation), sleep, eating and swilling, buttoning and unbuttoning – how much remains of downright existence?

The summer of a dormouse.

Lord Byron, journal entry for 7 December 1813

'My hero is Lord Byron. Don Juan is a comic masterpiece and he frequently mocked his own romantic image. His letters are the best ever written and this is my favourite quotation from him.'

ANDREW MOTION

Poet Laureate

John Keats

(1795–1821)

The imagination may be compared to Adam's dream – he awoke and found it true.

John Keats

On First Looking into Chapman's Homer

Much have I travelled in the realms of gold,
And many goodly states and kingdoms seen;
Round many western islands have I been
Which bards in fealty to Apollo hold.
Oft of one wide expanse had I been told
That deep-browed Homer ruled as his demesne;
Yet did I never breathe its pure serene
Till I heard Chapman speak out loud and bold:
Then felt I like some watcher of the skies
When a new planet swims into his ken;
Or like stout Cortez when with eagle eyes
He stared at the Pacific – and all his men
Looked at each other with a wild surmise –
Silent, upon a peak in Darien.

'I nominate John Keats as my hero – not just because he wrote some of the truest and most beautiful poetry in the language, but also because he was a magnificent human being: funny, kind, sensitive, energetic, entertaining, brave, wise and generous. The poems and letters bear all this out – so much so, I felt spoilt for choice when it came to selecting a single phrase and a poem to prove his greatness.'

THE RT HON. THE COUNTESS MOUNTBATTEN OF BURMA

Sir Francis Drake

(c. 1540–95)

It is not the beginning of any great enterprise, but the continuing of the same unto the end, until it be thoroughly finished, which yieldeth the true glory.

Sir Francis Drake

'I know that this was a favourite quotation of my father's as well as mine, and one that he always acted upon.'

¶ This quote also forms the essence of a prayer known as Drake's Prayer:

O Lord God, When Thou givest to Thy servants to endeavour any great matter, grant us to know that it is not the beginning, but the continuing of the same unto the end, until it be thoroughly finished, which yieldeth the true glory: through Him who for the finishing of Thy work laid down His life, our Redeemer Jesus Christ. Amen.

CARDINAL CORMAC MURPHY-O'CONNOR
Cardinal Archbishop of Westminster

St Thomas More
(1478–1535)

You cannot get to heaven in feather beds – it is not the way, for Our Lord went there through much pain and suffering, and should we not be like our Master?

St Thomas More

'I admire St Thomas More because of his steadfastness in troubled times and, above all, for his faithfulness to his conscience and to the Church.'

DR BASIL MUSTAFA
Fellow, Oxford Centre for Islamic Studies

S. Abul Hasan Ali Nadwi
(1914–99)

But what will the answer be if in this country which is bustling with life and activity one were to ask how many real men lived; men whose hearts throbbed and eyes wept for the sake of humanity; men who controlled their carnal desires and were the riders and not the mounts of this civilization; who held the reins of life instead of being driven by it; who knew their Creator and whose hearts were filled with love for Him and respect for mankind; who led a simple life in harmony with nature, and were aware of true joys and genuine pleasures; who did not like tensions and conflicts in the world and hated the selfishness and greed of the politicians; who wished every country well and wanted it to prosper; who were eager to give and not to grab . . . who saw gain in loss and victory in defeat . . . men who aspired to release humanity from the bondage of the inordinate appetites of power, wealth and even intellect?

S. Abul Hasan Ali Nadwi, from a speech delivered at the
Muslim Community Centre, Chicago, 19 June 1977

'S. Abul Hasan Ali Nadwi was an eminent scholar of Islam and a spiritual leader, a man of letters and an educator. He was universally admired and respected for his gracious manners and spiritual capacity. He taught in India at Lucknow, and was the author of more than 30 books.'

SIR PATRICK NAIRNE

Retired civil servant and academic

Sir Edmund Hillary

(1919–2008)

Great things are done when men and mountains meet. This is not done by jostling in the street.

William Blake, from *MS Notebooks*

'Although, of course not known to him, I am sure Blake would have approved of Hillary.'

Archbishop William Temple

(1881–1944)

People ask me whether I am not wearing myself out with all this speaking. The truth is that what wears one out is not what one does, but what one does not do.

Attributed to William Temple

'I admire this wise remark attributed to one of the greatest men of the Anglican Church.'

TIM NEWELL

Former Prison Governor, now working with victims of crime, and those who have offended against them

George Fox

(1624–91)

You will say, Christ saith this, and the apostles say this; but what canst thou say? Art thou a child of Light and hast thou walked in the Light, and what thou speakest is it inwardly from God?

George Fox

'In 1652 George Fox was exploring his ministry in discovering the basis of Quakerism, and these words provide the most challenging question for me about my own faith. In a few sentences Fox sums up all the responsibility to live my faith daily.

This is challenging at all times, not comfortable but inspirational – and the critical question for me is still: "What canst thou say?"'

WILCO PRESCOTT

Age 7, Lorretto Convent Junior School, Gibraltar

William Wallace

(*c.* 1275–1305)

William Wallace is a very good man,
In Scotland he was born in 1275.
Loving his people,
Loves helping his people.
In the night he had a fight,
And always tried his best.
My hero is William Wallace.

Wilco Prescott

SENATOR DAVID NORRIS

Senator, Seanad Éiran, Dublin

James Joyce

(1882–1941)

'When the character Leopold Bloom in Joyce's *Ulysses* is challenged about his ethnic origin as a Jew, he talks of Jesus Christ as a Jew and continues to maintain that the essence of life is not about an unending string of insults, arguments, hatred and history, but in fact is the opposite of that. When put under pressure he acknowledges that the essence to which he is referring is that of love; not just the love celebrated in sentimental verse but the ordinary domestic painstaking love that keeps society together throughout history.'

JOHN JULIUS NORWICH

Author and broadcaster

Freya Stark

(1893–1993)

Though it may be unessential to the imagination, travel is necessary to an understanding of men. Only with long experience and the opening of his wares on many a beach where his language is not spoken, will the merchant come to know the worth of what he carries, and what is parochial and what is universal in his choice. Such delicate goods as justice, love and honour, courtesy, and indeed all the things we care for, are valid everywhere; but they are variously moulded and often differently handled, and sometimes nearly unrecognizable if you meet them in a foreign land; and the art of learning fundamental common values is perhaps the greatest gain of travel to those who wish to live at ease among their fellows.

Freya Stark, from *Perseus in the Wind*

'Freya Stark is one of the wisest women I ever knew.'

Other contributors choosing Freya Stark are:

SERENA DE LA HEY, artist and sculptor in willow: 'There can be no happiness if the things we believe in are different from the things we do' (source unverified).

Also OLINDA ADEANE, journalist, 'The great and almost only comfort about being a woman is that one can always pretend to be more stupid than one is and no one is surprised' (from *The Valley of the Assassins*). 'I love travellers, especially those who take you with them on their journey, Freya Stark was brave in her personal life and rapier-witted in her writing.'

LADY NUNNELEY

Retired lecturer at the Victoria & Albert Museum

Julian Grenfell and others killed in the First World War

To Julian Grenfell

Because of you we will be glad and gay,
Remembering you we will be brave and strong;
And hail the advent of each dangerous day,
And meet the last adventure with a song.

And, as you proudly gave your jewelled gift,
We'll give our lesser offering with a smile,
Nor falter on that path where, all too swift,
You led the way and leapt the golden stile.

Whether new paths, new heights to climb you find,
Or gallop through the unfooted asphodel,
We know you know we shall not lag behind,
Nor halt to waste a moment on a fear;
And you will speed us onward with a cheer,
And wave beyond the stars that all is well.

Maurice Baring (1874–1945)

'I particularly like this poem because, although it is addressed to Julian
Grenfell, it is about all the beautiful young men who gave their lives
for their country in the First World War and, although many of them
are names known to us, many more died as unknown heroes and
should never be forgotten.'

❡ Julian Grenfell (1888–1915), author of the poem 'Into Battle', had been a
student at Eton ten years before Baring. He won the DSO in France and was
killed at Ypres.

GERALD O'COLLINS
Theologian

St Paul
(d. *c.* 65 CE)

As servants of God we prove ourselves in every way: through great endurance, in afflictions, troubles, difficulties, beatings, imprisonments, disorders, labours, sleepless nights, hunger . . . through honour and dishonour, in ill repute and good repute.

We are treated as imposters and yet are truthful; as unknown and yet well known; as dying and behold we live; as punished and never killed; as grieving but always rejoicing; as poor but enriching many; as having nothing and yet possessing all things.

2 Corinthians 6.4–5, 8–10, translated from the Greek by Gerald O'Collins

'We all experience our deep anxieties and persistent worries – about ourselves, our families, our country, our Church and our world. Whatever our sufferings and afflictions, Paul assures us in his second letter to the Corinthians, God will prove the unfailing source of true strength and real comfort. That is the wonderful, central message of Paul's most autobiographical letter.'

REVD JOHN OLIVER
Retired naval chaplain

St Polycarp
(*c.* 69–*c.* 155)

Fourscore and six years have I served Him, and he hath done me no wrong. How then can I blaspheme my King and my Saviour? If you require of me to swear by the genius of Caesar hear my free confession, I am a Christian.

St Polycarp, Bishop of Smyrna, in reply to the proconsul

'St Polycarp was an important figure in the life of the Church in Asia Minor, a disciple of St John the Evangelist and a member of the group known as the "Apostolic Fathers". He was arrested in Smyrna during the persecution of Marcus Aurelius, rejecting the chance to escape, saying, "God's will be done." He was led to the tribunal of the proconsul, who exhorted him to have regard for his age, swear by the genius of Caesar and to revile Christ. It is St Polycarp's reply that is a source of inspiration.

He was sentenced to be burned alive but refused to be bound, saying, "He who gives me grace to endure the fire will enable me to remain at the pile unmoved." The courage and faithfulness of a frail old man is a source of inspiration to one who seeks to lead a Christian life with minuscule martyrdoms that pale into insignificance in the light of St Polycarp.'

Dom Stephen Ortiger

Benedictine monk; former Abbot of Worth

St Benedict

(480–c. 547)

When they rise for the Night Office, let them gently encourage one another, on account of the excuses to which the sleepy are addicted. (RB 22)

We do, indeed, read that wine is no drink for monks; but since nowadays monks cannot be persuaded of this, let us at least agree upon this, to drink temperately and not to satiety: for *wine maketh even the wise to fall away.* (RB 40)

In administering correction, let the Abbot act with prudent moderation, lest being too zealous in removing the rust he break the vessel. (RB 64)

Let the Abbot so temper all things that the strong may still have something to long after, and the weak may not draw back in alarm. (RB 64)

St Benedict, The Rule of St Benedict, chapter 64,
translated by Abbot Justin McCann, 1995

'St Benedict is the patriarch of western monks. Only the Gospel is in League Division One, but St Benedict's "Little Rule for Beginners" is at the very top of League Division Two; it combines zeal for God with wisdom, moderation, gentle humour and compassion.'

GARETH OWEN

Writer and broadcaster

The 1st Earl of Clarendon

(1609–74)

The king is a suitor to you . . . that you will join with him in restoring the whole nation to its primitive temper and integrity, to its old good manners, its old good humour and its old good nature . . . If the old reproaches of 'cavalier' and 'roundhead' and 'malignant' be committed to the grave, let us not find more significant and better words to signify worse things . . . let not piety and godliness be measured by a morosity in manners . . . Very merry men have been very godly men, and if a good conscience be a continual feast, there is no reason but men be very merry at it.

Earl of Clarendon

'This speech was made by the Earl of Clarendon at the adjournment of Parliament in September 1660. As Edward Hyde, Clarendon accompanied the young Charles II into exile and at the restoration made this persuasive appeal for reconciliation following the rivening events of the Civil War. I love it for its utter lack of political rhetoric and bombast. His words are modest and reasonable and he speaks plainly and simply as a wise good-natured man might speak to another in quest of good sense and moderation. And it's wonderful English.'

❡ Gareth Owen has given a poetry performance for the Threshold Prize charity for children's writing, and here is a taste of his poetry . . .

Universal Zoo

The creatures of the world one day
Packed sandwiches and tea
And toured the Universal Zoo
To see what they could see.

And all alone in a tiny cage
Sat a child on an unmade bed
With the word 'Endangered Species' scrawled
On the wall above his head.

THE RT HON. THE LORD OWEN
Politician and statesman

Clive Gimson
(1919–82)

Once I Was Young

Once I was young
And filled with winged ideas,
With songs unsung
To echo down the years.

The old men smiled
'We sang those selfsame songs
Once on a time –
Convinced we could right all wrongs'.

Thinking them blind
I kept my faith unfurled:
Made up my mind
Youth would convert the world.

The years have passed
And I am older now,
Youth does not last,
The blossom leaves the bough.

Yet wiser now
I know a wider truth,
I have learned how
Hope is the spirit's youth.

Clive Gimson

'Clive Gimson, a devout but questioning Christian, was my form master in my first year at Bradfield College. He won a Military Cross in the Second World War, and lost part of a lung through tuberculosis, but still gained a Blue in Fives at Cambridge. He taught me to rock climb, and about patience – not one of my strengths.

He wrote to me, "One of the keys to all this is patience . . . If I had gone flat out to catch some particular bus, I am sure I would have become a real shyster – perhaps I am – because to achieve success it seems necessary to throw over many of the ideals of youth by trampling on the weak and putting oneself first."

We would often talk for four or five hours, hardly stopping for a meal. Once, when we talked about Rhodesia after a particularly frustrating negotiation I had just had with a recalcitrant Ian Smith, he forced me to think through what it all looked like, from the white settlers' viewpoint, desperate, as they faced defeat.'

Sir Christopher Paine

Oncologist and radiologist, retired chairman of the
Royal Society of Medicine

Rudyard Kipling

(1865–1936)

> Brethren how shall it fare with me
> When the war is laid aside,
> If it be proven that I am he
> For whom a world has died?
>
> Verse 1 from 'The Question'
> by Rudyard Kipling

'Kipling's war poems, although not always easy, reveal the deep emotions and real ethical difficulties of the First World War, linked no doubt to the sadness of his son John's enrolment and death.

'The Question' was written in 1916, a year after John Kipling's death at Loos and a year before America entered the war and after President Wilson had said, "There's such a thing as being too proud to fight".'

❡ Verse 5 from 'The Question' reads:

> If it be found, when the battle clears,
> Their death has set me free,
> Then how shall I live with myself through the years
> Which they have bought for me?

UNKNOWN SOLDIER

GEOFFREY PALMER

Actor

~≫ ≪~

T. C. Kingsmill Moore

(1893–1979)

To my wife
who made so many fears groundless,
so many dreams a reality
Dedication of his book, *A Man May Fish*

'Kingsmill Moore is not in truth a hero, nor did I ever meet him. But I have chosen him for the touching simplicity of this dedication.'

❡ An excerpt from *A Man May Fish*, chapter 1:

Fishing literature burst upon me when I went to Marlborough, for in the school library were all the standard works of the day. Not four hundred yards from where I sat reading, the Kennet glided under White Horse Hill, and though boys were not allowed to fish, no-one could bandage my eyes . . . I lay on my face and saw the bright beetles and all the scurrying insects of the grass roots crawl under me, stood waist deep in the water to dip out the hiding nymphs, watched them turn into duns and then, shedding their last film, into the crystal of the spinner. The wild duck led her string of ducklings down stream and never noticed me, the trout sucked in a dun or swirled more energetically after an escaping sedge within a few yards of where I sat motionless. It was a lesson in 'Study to be quiet'.

A Man May Fish, chapter 7:

The only time when experienced fishermen occasionally get their lines tangled is when fishing [from a boat] in the twilight and when this happens it is as well to remember how far sound travels over water.

Dr John Lloyd Parry

Dean of the Institute of Sports and Exercise Medicine

Henry Dunant

(1828–1910)

Tutti fratelli. (All are brothers).

I am a disciple of Christ, as in the first century, simply that.

Henry Dunant

'The indomitable courage and vision of one of the world's greatest humanitarians, ultimately to receive the Nobel Peace Prize, is an example both humbling and inspirational for me.'

❡ Dunant, by an accident of history while looking for a land concession from Emperor Napoleon III, happened to be present as a bystander at the battle of Solferino, in Lombardy in 1859. The casualties left on the battlefield were 40,000 dead and wounded. Dunant threw himself unprepared into three days of gruelling and horrific relief work. He returned to Geneva and wrote *A Memory of Solferino* which eventually led to the creation of the International Committee for the Relief of the Wounded, the future International Committee of the Red Cross. Dunant's career lurched from extreme fame to extreme poverty following a bankruptcy, and back to fame in his last years as joint winner of the first Nobel Peace Prize.

YTZACK ELKERBOUT BONICH

Age 6, Lorretto Convent Junior School, Gibraltar

Batman

I love Batman
because he is the best.
He has a rope
and he has lots of weapons

Batman is my hero
because he is strong
and he is never wrong.

Ytzack Elkerbout Bonich

HUGH PARRY

Adult education tutor

Thomas Fuller

(1608–61)

Lord, Be pleased to shake my Clay Cottage, before thou throwest it down. May it totter a while, before it doth Tumble. Let me be summon'd before I am surpriz'd. Deliver me from Sudden Death. Not from Sudden Death, in respect of itself, for I care not how short my passage be, so it be safe. Never any weary Traveller Complained, that he came too soon to his Journeys end. But let it not be Sudden in respect of me. Make me always ready to receive Death. Thus no Guest comes unawares to him, who keeps a Constant Table.

Thomas Fuller, from Good Thoughts in Bad Times

'The title of Fuller's book was apt. The times were bad, with bigotry and violence rampant. Fuller showed that piety was compatible with self-deprecation, laugh-aloud wittiness and a tolerant curiosity about everything that came his way.'

GENERAL SIR ROBERT PASCOE

Former Adjutant General, Late The Royal Green Jackets

Lawrence of Arabia

(1888–1935)

Do not try to do too much with your own hands. Better the Arabs do it tolerably than that you do it perfectly. It is their war, and you are to help them, not to win it for them. Actually, also, under the very odd conditions of Arabia, your practical work will not be as good as, perhaps, you think it is.

T. E. Lawrence, from *The Seven Pillars of Wisdom*

'Having read *Seven Pillars of Wisdom* as a young officer long ago and been fascinated by its author T. E. Lawrence, I went off to Lebanon and spent 18 months learning Arabic, intent on advancing my military career somewhere in the Middle East. The fates decreed otherwise, but my interest lingers on although much saddened by recent events in this fascinating but troubled region. I wonder what Lawrence would have made of it all?'

BRIAN PATTEN

Poet

Ralph Nelson

(1946–)

I was sitting on a riverbank
When a man came up to me and said
I should be earning a living,
I should be working hard instead,
Then when I'm old, if I'm rich and I wish
I could be sitting on a riverbank, fishing for fish.

Brian Patten on Ralph Nelson

'A little-known poet and trickster, Ralph Nelson's philosophy of life is one I greatly admire. He and his Japanese partner, Mitsuko, seem to live on air. Since I've known Ralph he's changed his name a few times so as not to be burdened. Ralph and Mitsuko have no permanent home and drift from place to place, settling for brief whiles in their favourite locations, then being blown on again like dandelion seeds.

They have no desire to earn money other than enough to buy wine and food for the day and they are now and then at the mercy of others' hospitality. If everyone followed their example civilization as we know it would probably collapse. But hey, heroes are rare creatures, and thank God for that. Life would be exhausting with too many of them. I wrote the above poem for Ralph around 2002 when I last saw him in a café in Marrakech.'

❡ Brian Patten has given a poetry performance for the Threshold Prize charity for children's writing, as have ADRIAN MITCHELL and GARETH OWEN.

THE RT HON. LORD PATTEN
Former Governor of Hong Kong

❦

St Thomas More
(1478–1535)

More is a man of an angel's wit and singular learning. I know not his fellow. For where is the man of that gentleness, lowliness and affability? And, as time requireth, a man of marvellous mirth and pastimes, and sometime of a sad gravity. A man for all seasons.

Robert Whittinton, writing about his contemporary, Sir Thomas More

'I think that with the Duke of Wellington, he is the greatest Englishman. You may recall that G. K. Chesterton regarded him as "the greatest historical character in English history", and that his comrade and friend Erasmus regarded him as "more pure than any snow". Erasmus added, "such as England never had and never again will have". The title of Robert Bolt's play about More, *The Man for All Seasons*, is taken from Robert Whittinton's account of him.'

RAMESH PATTNI

Business consultant and Chair of the Interfaith Committee of the
Hindu Forum of Britain

Swami Chinmayananda

(1916–93)

Strive, we must. We should not become doped like a tree or unconscious like a stone. We are human beings with intelligence and reason.

. . . Man refuses to learn, although Mother Nature and Father Life, day in and day out, tirelessly give us wise tuitions.

Swami Chinmayananda, from *Vedanta through Letters*

'Swami Chinmayananda, born Menon Balakrishna, whom I greatly admire, has been a powerful influence all my life.

A feature writer for the *National Herald* newspaper and with a wide education, he was involved in India's independence movement. During his convalescence following imprisonment and a life-threatening illness, he chanced upon some spiritual articles. Full of scepticism, he went to the Himalayas to seek out Swami Sivananda. But the young sceptic turned enthusiast and finally convert.

He took sanyasa from Swami Sivananda and was given the name Swami Chinmayananda. Later he studied under the tutelage of Swami Tapovanam, one of the great Vedantic masters.

In 1951, he decided to bring to all people the teaching of Vedanta, the non-dualist tradition of Hinduism, traditionally reserved for the priestly class. He both taught worldwide and established a network of Chinmaya Missions, hospitals, clinics, schools and temples.'

JULIAN PETTIFER

Broadcaster and writer

T. S. Eliot

(1888–1965)

So here I am, in the middle way, having had twenty years –
Twenty years largely wasted, the years of *l'entre deux guerres* –
Trying to learn to use words, and every attempt
Is a wholly new start, and a different kind of failure
Because one has only learnt to get the better of words
For the thing one no longer has to say, or the way in which
One is no longer disposed to say it. And so each venture
Is a new beginning, a raid on the inarticulate
With shabby equipment always deteriorating
In the general mess of imprecision of feeling,
Undisciplined squads of emotion. And what there is to conquer
By strength and submission, has already been discovered
Once or twice, or several times, by men whom one cannot hope
To emulate – but there is no competition –
There is only the fight to recover what has been lost
And found and lost again and again: and now, under conditions
That seem unpropitious. But perhaps neither gain nor loss.
For us, there is only the trying. The rest is not our business.

T. S. Eliot, from 'Four Quartets, East Coker, V'

'In my teens, T. S. Eliot aroused in me an interest in contemporary
poetry and inspired me to try to write. This quotation has always
seemed to me to state perfectly the dilemma and frustration of the
creative writer.'

¶ Julian Pettifer also chose John Donne.

~ * ~

William Shakespeare

(1564–1616)

> Cromwell, I charge thee, fling away ambition:
> By that sin fell the angels; how can man, then,
> The image of his Maker, hope to win by it?
>
> William Shakespeare, *King Henry VIII*, Act IV, Scene II

'Cardinal Wolsey is dying and counsels Thomas Cromwell, Henry's
henchman, who dissolved the first Coventry Cathedral among many
others in 1539, but lost his head for his pains.

When I was asked: "Bishop or Dean?" I replied, "Dean" and was
rewarded with the most interesting appointment in the Church of
England. Subsequently I was again approached but said that I would
rather stay in Coventry. Other rewards came, but most truly of all in
the style of the prayer, "and not to ask for any reward save that of
knowing that we do Thy will".

The other quote I have chosen is from *Hamlet*, Act I, Scene III:

> The friends thou hast, and their adoption tried,
> Grapple them to thy soul with hoops of steel;

These quotes illuminate why Shakespeare means so much to me. He
combines richness of insight with beauty of the English language
and humour, interlacing wisdom. Like Mozart and Michelangelo, in
their respective spheres, he is a genius.'

Thorold Coade

(1896–1963)

*The Dance**

I am sure what we need to learn is to live (sometimes, at all events) as these people dance. The ballroom dancer is not concerned to get from one end of the room to the other, the ballet dancer is not trying to cross the stage in record time. Each of them is moving to and fro, backwards and forwards, and often round in circles, in response to no call to get somewhere by a given time, but in response to an inner rhythm interpreted for him or her by the music. It is like that if we want to learn to move in harmony with the beauty, with the purpose, with the will of God. If we can live at times like that, we begin to feel a new and a true sense of balance; we begin to breathe another air. And by degrees we begin to find that life is quite a different thing from what we had imagined, it begins to make sense. And this realization slowly begins to alter the texture of our lives, and shift our standard of values on to a surer basis.

Thorold Coade, from *The Burning Bow*

'This is an extract from a talk – or perhaps sermon – by Thorold Coade entitled 'The Dance'. Coade was the inspirational headmaster of Bryanston School when I was a pupil there.'

❡ *Sometimes curiously titled, 'On "The Dance".'

Robby Lantz

The boat may not leave on time but it does go more than once.

Robby Lantz

'This was said to me by Robby Lantz in that wonderful Mittel European accent of his when I asked him about an actress whose career had started in stellar fashion but had apparently come to an end. I love that sentiment. When things are really going well they can just stop. And more importantly, in the middle of an unlikely grey day, the sun can come through.'

SIR MATTHEW PINSENT

Olympic Gold Medallist oarsman

Ernest Shackleton

(1874–1922)

We had seen God in His splendours, heard the text that Nature renders. We had reached the naked soul of man.

Ernest Shackleton

'He was an extraordinary leader, explorer and survivor, a product of his age and ambition; his type is almost extinct in the modern world. From afar I can only guess at the qualities that led him to drive himself and his men through the jeopardy and difficulties that beset them. He makes sport at any level seem trivial.'

ADAM POLLOCK

Impresario

Stephen Oliver

(1950–92)

It's only money.

Stephen Oliver

'Stephen Oliver's frequent use of this dismissive phrase encapsulates his
exceptional generosity, and the life-enhancing use he made of his
considerable earnings as a successful composer. He lived an almost
monk-like existence in bare rooms, devoting his life to writing music
and helping others – funding small-scale opera companies, chamber
groups, young musicians and, often, simply people in need. He
valued the blessing of friendship above all else, and not surprisingly
his last major work was an opera based on Timon of Athens for
E.N.O.'

❡ As well as a symphony and several chamber pieces, Stephen Oliver wrote 40
operas, including *The Duchess of Malfi*, *Tom Jones*, *Euridice*, *Beauty and the
Beast*, *Mario and the Magician*, *Timon of Athens*, *L'Oca del Cairo*, as well as many
scores for the theatre, film and TV such as *The Lord of the Rings*, *Nicholas Nick-
leby* and *Peter Pan*.

THE HON. SIR JONATHON PORRITT

Environmentalist, former Director of Friends of the Earth

Hildegard of Bingen

(1098–1179)

The Word is living, being, spirit, all verdant greening, all creativity.
This Word manifests itself in every living creature.

Hildegard of Bingen, from Hildegardis Scivias
(ed. Adelgundis Fuhrkotter, Corpus Christianorum Continuatio Mediaevalis)

'I first encountered Hildegard of Bingen's work in 1983, courtesy of Matthew Fox's wonderful book *Original Blessing: A Primary in Creation Spirituality*. Throughout her life, she was a passionate defender of the natural world ("The Earth must not be injured, the Earth must not be destroyed"), and an equally passionate celebrant of what she called "viriditas", the Greening power of God revealed in every nook and cranny of creation. There is such power and truth in her work; and in the rather dry, often narrowly secular world of the modern environment movement she has been a constant source of inspiration to me – in the sure knowledge that those who do indeed see every living thing as a "word of God" are less inclined to trash the natural world in the way we are still doing today.'

¶ Hildegard of Bingen was a Benedictine Abbess, medieval mystic and visionary whose community was at Rupertsberg, near Bingen on the Rhine. Her visions spoke of light 'more brilliant than the sun, . . . and I name it "the cloud of the living light" . . . Sometimes I behold within this light another light which I name "the living light itself", and when I look on it, every sadness and pain vanishes from my memory.' She saw women and men as equal in their work for God in the 'creative greenness' of his spirit. Writer, artist, healer and musician, she illustrated her own books, wrote a *vade mecum*, *The Book of Simple Medicine*, composed a symphonia with many song settings, and wrote more than 80 melodies for a morality play.

PROFESSOR SIR GHILLEAN PRANCE

Former Director of Kew Gardens

George Perkins Marsh

(1801–82)

. . . Man is everywhere a disturbing agent. Wherever he plants his foot, the harmonies of nature are turned to discords. The proportions and accommodations which insured the stability of existing arrangements are overthrown. Indigenous vegetable and animal species are extirpated, and supplanted by others of foreign origin . . .

There are, indeed, brute destroyers, beast and birds and insects of prey – all animal life feeds upon, and, of course, destroys other life,

– but this destruction is balanced by compensations . . . Man pursues his victims with reckless destructiveness: and, while the sacrifice of life by lower animals is limited by the cravings of appetite, he unsparingly persecutes, even to extirpation, thousands of organic forms which he cannot consume.

> George Perkins Marsh, from *Man and Nature: Or, Physical Geography as Modified by Human Action*, edited by David Lowenthal

'George Perkins Marsh was a remarkable prophet who, in 1864, was writing about ecology with a profound understanding long before that term was created, and his words resonate with today's environmental crisis. I often consult his book and wonder why the world took little notice of his wisdom until recently when it is almost too late. Marsh in some ways was, along with other prophets, a founder of the conservation movement. His book shows a deep concern about the way in which nature is being devastated by humans.'

SENATOR FEARGAL QUINN

Senator and company director

~ ~

Masatoshi Ito

(1925–)

Whether you believe you can
Or whether you believe you can't
You are right.

> Masatoshi Ito, possibly quoting from an earlier sage

'Masatoshi Ito is a great Japanese retailer whom I've come to admire. He started his company in 1952, and when I started mine in 1960 he still had one shop. When we last spoke, his company had over 10,000 stores. I asked him how he succeeded, and this was what he said.'

¶ Masatoshi Ito is Founder and Honorary Chairman of the Seven & I Holdings Co. Ltd, Tokyo, Japan.

~ ~

P. H. C. Cavanagh

(1888–?)

The Revd E. F. Habershon

(1886–1982)

From *To Anthea, Who May Command Him Anything*

Bid me to live, and I will live
Thy Protestant to be;
Or bid me love, and I will give
A loving heart to thee.

A heart as soft, a heart as kind,
A heart as sound and free
As in the whole world thou can find;
That heart I'll give to thee.

. . .

Thou art my life, my love, my heart,
The very eyes of me:
And has command of every part
To live and die for thee.

Revd Robert Herrick (1591–1674)

'This is the poem I first learned with two schoolmasters of mine. P. H. C. Cavanagh taught me Classics and English. He had no pretensions to scholarship, yet when he went to war in 1914, Horace and Virgil went with him. The other, the Revd E. F. Habershon, came to read poetry with us and teach us cricket or, since I was no cricketer, a lot about birds, butterflies and wild flowers.

They left behind them an abiding sense of Englishness and gratitude for their example of gentle kindliness, together with a love of the subjects they taught me.

The poem is doubly precious now as I discovered recently that my wife had, at some time, pencilled my initial and a kiss in the margin beside it in my anthology; and it is she who is the real heroine of my life.'

THE RT HON. THE LORD RAMSBOTHAM

The Revd P. H. (Val) Rogers

(1912–2001)

'WHY?'

Revd P. H. (Val) Rogers

'Throughout my years at Haileybury I was fortunate enough to be taught English by a remarkable man. Val Rogers, assistant chaplain, notable oarsman and distinguished English scholar, was a friend of that outstanding group of writers which included Auden, Isherwood, Fry, MacNeice and Eliot.

During the Second World War, though initially a pacifist, when his beloved brother was killed at Dunkirk, he joined up. Wounded in Italy, while recovering he was much influenced by the Abbot of the monastery at Assisi, going on to be ordained in the Anglican Church.

From the start he made it clear that his principal weapon was the word "Why". He took us on literary journeys, exploring the highways

and byways of poetry and prose, to ensure that we had a wide background on which to base our studies. No pupil's statement went unchallenged and we were expected to challenge him. We enjoyed his enjoyment of tilting with reactionary windmills, such as my housemaster, who regarded him as a bad influence and a dangerous rebel.

When I was appointed Her Majesty's Chief Inspector of Prisons, Val wrote to me, reflecting on the sort of challenges I might discover. I was glad that, shortly before he died, I was able to tell him how invaluable his weapon was proving and how often I heard his infectious laugh when I used it against an unjustified assertion.'

DR DAVID RAWLINS

Former doctor to and leader for the Ramblers' Association for the Himalayas; co-founder of Somerset Accident Voluntary Emergency Service

St Photini

(?AD 1–?AD 60)

Whosoever drinketh of the water that I shall give him shall never thirst; but the water that I shall give him shall be in him a well of water springing up into everlasting life.

The woman saith unto him, Sir, give me this water, that I thirst not.

John 4.14–15

'I first came across the name Photini while in Greece; she was the daughter of the owners of a hotel I have stayed at on a number of occasions in Samos. Later I noticed on the map a couple of villages called Agia Photini (St Photini), both in Crete. The name is sometimes transliterated as Fotini. I realized that most Greeks are given the name of a saint, so intrigued, never having heard the name before, I started to research her.

St John (4.5–42) describes how Jesus was resting by a deep well in Samaria, and as he had no bucket he asked a Samaritan woman to draw him some water. This request surprised her. After some conversation, which included the revelation that her private life was no secret to him, she came to believe that he was the Messiah, and many Samaritans in that town came to that belief.

According to Orthodox tradition she, with her five sisters and two sons, were baptized at Pentecost, taking the name Photini (which means "enlightened"). She travelled widely in Asia, North Africa and Europe, surpassing many of the male disciples and evangelists in spreading Christianity. In Rome, Nero imprisoned her, and while there she died, after having converted his daughter Domina (and her slaves and servants), thus infuriating him.'

MOHAMMAD SHAHID RAZA

Director, Imams and Mosques Council UK, Executive Secretary of
the Muslim Law (Shariah) Council UK

Ali ibn Abi Talib

(598–661 AD)

One who recognizes himself, recognizes the creator.

Fear of Allah makes one feel secure.

Learned men live even after death, whilst the ignorant are dead although alive.

Ali ibn Abi Talib

'Ali ibn Abi Talib is highly revered by both Sunni and Shia Muslims, and the Sufis consider him as the fountainhead of their spiritual doctrine. Historically he is remembered for his piety, nobility, learning and bravery, and as such he is often referred to as "The Lion of Allah" and "The Gate of Knowledge". He is a cousin of Prophet Muhammad (PUBH) and the fourth Caliph and was the first young person to accept Islam. Other quotations from him include, "Better alone than in bad company" and "One who perceives himself as the best is actually the worst".'

Terry Waite CBE

(1939–)

I turned the card over and there was a message from someone I didn't know simply saying, 'We remember, we shall not forget, we shall continue to pray for you and to work for all people who are detained around the world.' I can tell you, that thought sent me back to the marvellous work of agencies like Amnesty International and their letter-writing campaigns. I would say to you all, never despise these simple actions. Something, somewhere, will get through to me and to my fellow hostages eventually.

Terry Waite, from *Taken on Trust*

'Some of the best moments in my life have been with Terry Waite. In early 2004 my brother and I asked him to join us and some relatives of British prisoners in Guantanamo, to campaign in Washington for the release to Britain of these men. All innocent, and all released since. Terry was held hostage in the Lebanon, in solitary confinement for four years, in chains for 1,763 days, so he spoke with a unique authority and was listened to with respect.'

JOHN REID

Retired flat-race jockey and racing manager

Johnny Reid

(1888–1984)

Be a good boy and keep out of bad company.

Johnny Reid

'My Grandfather Johnny Reid's one and only letter to me on my seventeenth birthday. He was a farmer in Northern Ireland and a horse owner/breeder and well respected for his knowledge of horses.'

Theo Green

(1925–1999)

If jockeys sat still, the horses would run faster.

Theo Green

'Theo Green was a prominent Australian racehorse trainer, and he also trained apprentice jockeys. Several of these became successful riders and won many big races in Australia, including numerous Sydney jockey premierships. He was a role model to the whole industry and is honoured by the Theo Green medal, which is awarded to the Sydney Champion Apprentice of each year.'

SIR WILLIAM REID

Retired ombudsman

George Herbert

(1593–1633)

The Church Porch

Judge not the preacher; for he is thy Judge:
If thou mislike him, thou conceiv'st him not.

God calleth preaching folly. Do not grudge
To pick out treasures from an earthen pot.
The worst speak something good: if all want sense,
God takes a text, and preaches patience.

Verse 70

'Herbert was the Public Orator for Cambridge University. He wrote the hymns "King of Glory, King of Peace" and "Teach Me, My God and King", and much verse. His best prose work is *A Priest to the Temple* – a shrewd guide to the work and life of the country clergyman he became. His use of words such as "the cream of all my heart" or "a glass of blessings" is striking, and I treasure his writings.'

SIR CLIFF RICHARD
Singer

Dr Billy Graham
(1918–)

Just as I am, without one plea
But that thy blood was shed of me,
And that thou bidd'st me come to thee,
O Lamb of God, I come.

Just as I am, thou wilt receive,
Wilt welcome, pardon, cleanse, relieve,
Because thy promise I believe:
O Lamb of God, I come.

Just as I am, of that free love
The breadth, length, depth, and height to prove,
Here for a season, then above:
O Lamb of God, I come. *

Charlotte Elliot (1789–1871)

'When I first read about the evangelist Billy Graham I was sceptical. I did not expect, when invited to talk about my Christian faith at an Earl's Court crusade meeting in 1966, to encounter a man who was to become a personal role model – someone I've admired and respected for nearly 40 years.

Within minutes of Billy starting his address, any lingering uncertainty evaporated and I was enthralled by the conviction, the power and the simple clarity of the man.

Critics say the whole phenomenon is shallow exploitation. I didn't think so then, and certainly not later when I had the privilege of getting to know Dr Graham personally through crusade meetings around the world.

Throughout the years, Billy has maintained a consistent integrity and Christian witness. He has won the respect of leaders the world over. There are countless thousands whose lives have been transformed after responding to Billy's invitation to "come to Christ".

Today Dr Graham is sick and frail. His beloved wife, Ruth, died in spring 2007. When he passes on himself, I'll be among the millions who will thank God for Billy Graham, his remarkable gifts, and a life lived simply and steadfastly to share the news of the Christian gospel.'

¶ *This is a hymn often sung at Billy Graham's crusade meetings.

ANDREW ROBERTS

Historian

Sir Winston Churchill

(1874–1965)

I am prepared to meet my Maker. Whether my Maker is prepared for the great ordeal of meeting me is another matter.

Winston Churchill, spoken at a news conference in Washington in 1954

'Although largely self-taught, Churchill had a penetrating intelligence which he exhibited constantly through his writings – he won the Nobel Prize for Literature – and his speeches, which continue to inspire us even four decades after his death.'

George Washington

(1732–99)

Happiness and moral duty are inseparably connected.

George Washington

'I would name George Washington, the first President of the United States, as a hero. Although at the outset a rebel and insurgent leader, he was a virtuous man who never betrayed his Christian ideals. He believed that religious belief was essential to the good conduct of government, and he always tried to conduct the rebellion against the British in as civilized a way as possible with regard to the treatment of prisoners and the prevention of atrocities.'

CANON ROGER ROYLE

Writer and broadcaster

Dame Cicely Saunders

(1918–2005)

People matter.

Dame Cicely Saunders

'Dame Cicely Saunders, the founder of the hospice movement, believed that no human life, however wretched, should be denied dignity and love. It was from her own experience of life and partly from her deep Christian faith that Dame Cicely became committed to the transformation of suffering. She was a powerful and practical visionary who changed our understanding of what it is to die a good death as she pioneered palliative care and saw this new medical discipline taken up in many parts of the world.

Dame Cicely recognized that hospices create "communities of the unlike". So I always give thanks for this remarkable person.'

Adapted from words used at her Thanksgiving Service in Westminster Abbey, 2006

✿

Viktor Frankl

(1905–97)

We who lived in concentration camps can remember the men who walked through the huts comforting others, giving away their last piece of bread. They may have been few in number, but they offer sufficient proof that everything can be taken away from a man but one thing: the last of the human freedoms – to choose one's attitude in any given set of circumstances, to choose one's own way.

Viktor Frankl, from *Man's Search for Meaning*

'For me, one of the heroes of the human spirit was Viktor Frankl, who survived Auschwitz, Dachau and other concentration camps, and helped others to survive. On the basis of his experiences he founded a new school of psychotherapy – he called it Logotherapy – the central idea of which is summed up in the title of his most famous book, *Man's Search for Meaning.*

Frankl rescued people from despair by helping them find a reason to live: a task not yet completed, work still to be done. That sense of a mission not yet fulfilled gave people the strength to carry on. In the quotation I chose [above] he bore witness to the courage of others. He also wrote of how, exhausted, starved and on the brink of death, he brought himself back to life by thinking of his beloved, his wife: "Then I grasped the meaning of the greatest secret that human poetry and human thought and belief have to impart: the salvation of man is through love and in love. I understood how a man who has nothing left in this world may still know bliss, be it only for a brief moment, in the contemplation of his beloved. For the first time in my life I was able to understand the meaning of the words, 'The angels are lost in perpetual contemplation of an infinite glory.'"

I am lost in admiration for a man who saved the lives of others by giving them hope, and who found a path to heaven at the very gates of hell.'

ELIZABETH MORENO

Age 11, Lorretto Convent Junior School, Gibraltar

Elizabeth, Princess of Hungary

(1207–1231)

She was the Princess of Hungary.
At the age of thirteen she married.
I like her name because it's mine.
Never hurt a soul,
Treated the poor and sick often.

Elizabeth gave her money to the poor,
Later she gave her time.
In her late twenties when it happened,
Zig Zag, she zoomed around helping the poor.
A baby she had, then three more,
Bread she fed to the poor.
Elizabeth died in 1231,
They loved her and called her 'Dear Elizabeth'.
Her last words were 'O Mary, come to help me.'

Elizabeth Moreno

SALEEF

Asylum seeker

My Father

Fù nkùket na nguet ouyì ndà suùnpu
(It is during a hard moment that you know your best friend.)

Fù mbga ntap bi boutnì
(Lost time is never found again.)

'My father used to use these expressions.'

¶ Saleef also gave me this strange quotation:

Ngnouee nà mbe numu, ou nté luluot
(If a snake bites you, you run away when you see a lizard.)

Saleef is a victim of torture and for him the slightest shock can bring back
terrifying thoughts so that lizards do indeed seem like snakes.

THE RT REVD MARK SANTER
Former Bishop of Birmingham

St Francis of Assisi
(1181–1226)

Where there is charity and wisdom
there is neither fear nor ignorance.
Where there is patience and humility
there is neither anger nor disturbance.
Where there is poverty with joy
there is neither covetousness nor avarice.
Where there is inner peace and meditation
there is neither anxiousness nor dissipation.
Where there is the fear of the Lord to guard the house,
there the enemy cannot gain entry.
Where there is mercy and discernment,
there is neither excess nor hardness of heart.

St Francis of Assisi, from *The Admonitions of Francis of Assisi:
Francis and Clare – The Complete Works*

'Francis speaks to us still because, like no other Christian we know
about, he embodies in his life as well as his teaching the demanding
tenderness of Jesus himself.'

JEHANGIR SAROSH

President of World Conference of Religions for Peace (Europe)

Mawlānā Jalāl al-Dīn Rūmī

(1207–73) (AH 604–72)

The Heart: Threshold Between Two Worlds

The five spiritual senses are connected.
They've grown from one root.
As one grows strong, the others strengthen too:
each one becomes a cupbearer to the rest.
Seeing with the eye increases speech;
speech increases discernment in the eye.
As sight deepens, it awakens every sense,
so that perception of the spiritual
becomes familiar to them all.
When one sense grows into freedom,
all the other senses change as well.
When one sense perceives the hidden,
the invisible world becomes apparent to the whole.

Mawlānā Jalāl al-Dīn Rūmī, from *Mathnawi II*, 3236–41

'As a Zoroastrian, Mawlānā Jalāl al-Dīn Rūmī reminds me of what
Zarathushtra taught about our own responsibility, our freedom to
choose to be connected. After all, the word religion (*relegio*) means
to reconnect. He speaks in simple language and binds the spirit of
the ultimate with the reality of the creation in harmony with the
Spirit of Man.

The mystic removes the mystery of the relation of the good creator
with the good creation and has the ability to merge the ultimate light
with the light of Man, offering the common union of the two for the
true communion.

By opening the senses through the heart, he reconnects us to the
ultimate, to each other and to mother earth. What more can you ask
for?'

David Schreiber

Candlemaker and retired art dealer

Sufi writers

(Eighth century AD)

In a public square one day, some people were shouting:

'Down with the Throne!'

They were faced by a party of Royal Guards, who were trying to beat them and take them prisoner.

Sufi Zafrandoz, accompanied by a few students, was watching the scene.

'Which party should we aid?' asked a pupil.

'The cripples!' said Zafrandoz.

'Which are cripples?'

'Both. The one party is incapable of ceasing to oppose authority. The other is unable to cease opposing them.'

'People handicapped in such a manner are in the grip of a disability which hampers them. They are crippled in thought as surely as a lame man is crippled in body. Why, therefore, do we feel sorry for, and try to help, only the physically handicapped who are such a minority?'

Tit for tat

Nasrudin went into a shop to buy a pair of trousers. Then he changed his mind and chose a cloak instead, at the same price.

Picking up the cloak he left the shop.

'You have not paid,' shouted the merchant.

'I left you the trousers, which were of the same value as the cloak.'

'But you did not pay for the trousers either.'

'Of *course* not,' said the Mulla – 'why should I pay for something that I did not want to buy?'

'I have long admired the Sufi writers, and the abundance of Sufi stories published in English during the last 50 years is quite extraordinary. The wisdom and humour of their stories encourage one to laugh sometimes, think sometimes, and to lean forward in anticipation of what is coming next.'

¶ The Sufis first appeared in Arabia in the eighth century. Although their roots are in the Islamic faith, they have links with Jewish, Christian, Buddhist and Animist origins. Deeply committed to God, they resist the tyrannical, ridicule the cruel, rich and merciless, exalt the low and help the helpless. Their literature ranges from poetry of great beauty, to humorous parables. Some of the protagonists in the stories, such as Nasrudin, though highly regarded may yet be apocryphal. Nasrudin, who is reputed to have been Tamerlaine's jester, has graves in several countries in Europe and the Middle East.

ROBERT SCOTT

Resident land agent, Co. Tyrone; Chairman, Forestry & Timber Association, 2002–4

Mikhail Gorbachev

(1931–)

I believe in the cosmos. All of us are linked to the cosmos. So nature is my god. To me nature is sacred. Trees are my temples and forests are my cathedrals.

'Mikhail Gorbachev had such a positive influence on the world that he surely deserves to be nominated as a hero. His reference to trees and forests struck a chord with me. One-fifth of the world's forests grow in Russia and the nurture of trees has played a large part in my life.'

St Joan of Arc

(1412–31)

Si je n'y suis pas, que Dieu m'y mette; si j'y suis, que Dieu m'y
tienne.
(If I am not there, may God so place me; if I am there, may God so
keep me.)

St Joan of Arc

'Saint Joan of Arc's devotion to her country and its cause was exceeded
only by her devotion to God. All her recorded responses at her trial
are of an unmatched dignity and purity, but I take particular comfort
from this quotation which forms her reply to the question whether
she stands in the Grace of God.'

¶ St Joan of Arc was also chosen by MICHAEL MORPURGO, writer and former
Children's Laureate, who emphasized her courage, faith and determination; and
that, despite being only 17 years old and illiterate, she managed to persuade the
French court, Dauphin and Army that she was the one to drive the English out
of France and that when faced with death she only weakened once, thinking she
could save herself from the flames, then withdrew her recantation and was
burned.

Joan was born in the village of Domrémy, in Lorraine. In 1425, during the
time of the Hundred Years War with the English and Civil War between the
houses of Orléans and Burgundy, she received a number of supernatural visita-
tions from St Michael, St Catherine and St Margaret telling her to lift the siege
at Orléans. Though she had no military knowledge and did not even know how
to ride, she responded and under her leadership the English were forced to lift
the siege of Orléans. However, Joan was subsequently sold to the English by the
Duke of Burgundy, tried and burned as a heretic in Rouen.

Dr John Sentamu

The Most Revd the Lord Archbishop of York

Archbishop Oscar Romero

(1917–80)

Peace will flower when love and justice pervade our environment.

Archbishop Oscar Romero

'Around my neck I wear a cross which bears these words of Archbishop Romero's.'

❡ Archbishop Oscar Arnulfo Romero of El Salvador was assassinated in 1980. He had a mission of outspoken commitment to those with no voice of their own and, despite pressure from the Vatican not to disturb the political *status quo*, he continued denouncing atrocities. He was killed as he said Mass in the chapel of the Divine Providence Hospital where he lived.

Judy Shercliff

Volunteer cathedral guide

Thomas Ken

(1637–1711); Bishop of Bath & Wells from 1684

God our Heavenly Father make, we pray, the door of this Cathedral Church wide enough to welcome all who need human love and fellowship and a Father's care; but narrow enough to shut out all envy, pride and lack of love. Here may the tempted find help, the sorrowing receive comfort, and the penitent be assured of your mercy; and here may all your children renew their strength and go on their way in hope and joy; through Jesus Christ our Lord. Amen.

'This prayer is often used in Wells Cathedral and I came to know it and Bishop Thomas Ken through being a guide there. The Ken family came from Cleveden, Somerset. However, Thomas, being an orphan, was reared by his half-sister and her husband Izaak Walton (of fishing fame).

Ordained in 1662, Bishop Ken was a loyal and principled priest; one of only a few Naval chaplains to become a bishop. He was also chaplain to Princess Mary in the Hague, but having sworn allegiance to James II was among the seven dissenting bishops* who would not swear allegiance to King William of Orange when he and Mary came to take the throne. Deprived of his see, he spent his remaining 20 years living in seclusion at Longleat in Wiltshire but was buried back in Somerset.

Ken's compassion for the suffering and destitute knew no bounds, and after Monmouth's defeat at the battle of Sedgemoor he tended to the needs of the prisoners awaiting trial by Judge Jeffreys in the Bloody Assizes in Somerset, and of Monmouth himself before his execution at the Tower of London. He must have thought his charity was overstretched when, at an earlier date, he baulked at giving Nell Gwynne hospitality during a court visit by Charles II.'

¶ *Bishop Trelawney of Cornwall and the Bishop of Bristol were also among those seven.

SIMON SHERCLIFF

Diplomat in Kabul; former VSO teacher in Tanzania

Sir Edmund Hillary

(1919–2008)

Climbing partners climb as one.

Edmund Hillary's comments on his and Tenzing's achievement

'I have known about the first ascent of Everest, by Hillary and Tenzing, for as long as I can remember. It happened well before I was born, but the picture taken by Hillary of Tenzing standing astride the roof of the world is timeless. The many fatal attempts on the summit illustrate the extreme human ambition and endeavour necessary in those hostile conditions. Tough and motivated, but straightforward, decent and modest, Hillary had the drive and self-belief necessary for the climb. He used his fame to help the country which made his name, setting up the Himalayan Trust which helps the Sherpa communities with developmental programmes. A real hero: he achieved legendary feats, yet always put others first.'

DAME STEPHANIE SHIRLEY
Pioneering IT entrepreneur

John Wesley
(1703–91)

Do all the good you can,
In all the ways you can,
In all the places you can,
At all the times you can,
To all the people you can,
As long as you ever can.

John Wesley, from *Rules of Conduct*

'This quote inspires me to give with joy.'

¶ John Wesley, the founder of the Methodist Church – a society which ministered to outsiders and the outcast – was the brother of Charles and uncle to Benjamin and the younger Charles. A scholar, preacher, organizer and man of action, he travelled over 250,000 miles, wrote 233 original works and preached over 40,000 sermons. He said in a letter in 1777, 'Though I am always in haste, I am never in a hurry.'

The Shirley Foundation supports medical research into Autism Spectrum Disorders.

MAJOR GENERAL RICHARD SHIRREFF

General Officer Commanding 3rd (United Kingdom) Division

Lawrence of Arabia

(1888–1935)

The greatest commander of men was he whose intuitions most nearly happened. Nine-tenths of tactics was certain enough to be teachable in schools; but the irrational tenth was like a kingfisher flashing across the pool, and in it lay the test of generals. It could be ensured only by instinct (sharpened by thought practising the stroke) until at the crisis it came naturally, a reflex.

T. E. Lawrence, from *The Seven Pillars of Wisdom*

'Lawrence was a scholar, historian, archaeologist, desert traveller of extraordinary endurance, Arabist and writer of at times almost biblical prose. Though not a professional soldier, he was a remarkable exponent of guerrilla and general warfare. I kept a copy of *The Seven Pillars* close at hand throughout my tour in Iraq, and turned to it almost daily. For me, the quotation is about more than generalship: it is about training, education, persistence and making your own luck. It is above all about boldness and taking the high-risk route, which usually yields the greatest dividend, rather than the safe lane.'

❧ Lawrence of Arabia was also chosen by KATHY SULLIVAN, astronaut.

DENNIS SILK

Retired headmaster, and former President of MCC and the TCCB

Archbishop Thomas Cranmer

(1489–1556)

Lighten our darkness, we beseech thee, O Lord; and by thy great mercy defend us from all perils and dangers of this night; for the sake of thy only Son, our Saviour, Jesus Christ. Amen.

Archbishop Thomas Cranmer, from the *Book of Common Prayer* (1662): Evening Prayer

'My favourite saint was, in fact, never an official saint at all, despite being burned at the stake. Thomas Cranmer wins my accolade for his services to the English language. He ranks with Tyndale and Shakespeare as being among the most influential forces of all time in forging the English language that was to become, by common consent, the *lingua franca* of the world. His natural feel for English prose dictated the direction of our English language for more than 400 years. His prayers coincided with the arrival of the printing press and were disseminated more widely than had ever been possible for a population who went unquestioning to church. It was Cranmer's Book of Common Prayer which decided what "good English" was. He was master of the sound of words and of sentence construction. He was prepared to use felicitous phrases from the works of anyone he wished. As one modern scholar has put it, "Cranmer's language lies at the heart of our own English-speaking culture, which has now become so central to the destiny of the world." We may criticize his theology and his political views. We may think Latimer and Ridley braver in the face of death than a man who had recanted five times. But his triumph over fear at the stake underlines his humanity. No cry escaped his lips as he stretched out his right hand "that hath offended" into the flames. We can identify with that.'

Sir Donald Sinden

Actor

The Battle of Britain pilots

Never in the field of human conflict was so much owed by so many to so few.

Sir Winston Churchill, following the Battle of Britain, 20 August 1940

'But for those few pilots of the RAF who, in 1940, defeated the German Luftwaffe, we many would not have enjoyed for so long the freedoms which are now being eroded by so few.'

Dr Indarjit Singh
Writer and broadcaster

Guru Arjan, the fifth Sikh Guru
(1563–1606)

A hundred shining vessels
Reflect the same bright light.
They may be broken
But the Sky will still remain.

Guru Arjan, from the *Guru Granth Sahib*, p. 736

'Guru Arjan was the founder of the Golden Temple in Amritsar and a pioneer of interfaith understanding. He lived at a time of acute religious conflict. The Guru declared that our different religions are different ways of looking at the same one God of us all; reflections of the one Reality behind all that exists, and that all faiths should be respected.

To show this respect, the Guru invited a famous Muslim saint to lay the foundation stone of the Golden Temple and constructed doors at each of its four sides to welcome visitors from any spiritual or geographical direction Guru Granth Sahib. He also included verses by Hindu and Muslim saints in the Sikh Holy Scriptures, which he compiled to show that no one faith had a monopoly of truth.

All this proved too much for the bigoted Mogul rulers, and the Guru was tortured to death, becoming the world's first martyr in the cause of interfaith understanding.'

❡ Guru Arjan was also selected by Charanjit Ajit Singh, Chairman for the International Interfaith Centre, who chose:

Of all good deeds
The best deed is
To meditate on the Name
And praise it for ever.

Of all speeches
The best speech is
To listen to and
Then reflect on God with others.

From Guru Arjan, from the *Sukhmani Sahib* (or Psalm of Peace and Happiness), 3:8. 'These verses, which I have often used in interfaith gatherings, make me think about the real purpose of religion. I feel that we need to come back to what it is that makes us all human and to view ourselves as spiritual beings in whom the same divine light pervades.'

ISABELLE EDWARDS

Age 6, Lorretto Convent Junior School, Gibraltar

My Heroine

I love my Granny
Because she is fantastic.
She is fun and she
Is the best cookie maker.

She is the best Granny.
She saves me and my sister
And she will save you if you
Fall off the fridge or the bunk-bed.

Isabelle Edwards

CHRISTINA SLADE

Professor of Media Theory at Utrecht University, and
Dean of Humanities at Macquarie University, Sydney

David Malouf

(1934–)

He is, they tell me, the one surviving speaker of his tongue. Half a century back, when he was a boy, the last of his people were massacred. The language, one of hundreds, died with them. Only not quite. For all his lifetime this man has spoken it, if only to himself. The words, the great system of sound and silence (for all languages, even the simplest, are a great and complex system) are locked up now in his heavy skull, behind the folds of the black brow . . . when he narrows his eyes, and grins and says 'Yes, boss, you wanna see me?', it is not breathed out . . .

David Malouf, from *The Only Speaker of his Tongue*

'David Malouf, an Australian writer of Lebanese descent, delivered the Boyer Lectures (the equivalent of the Reith Lectures) on ABC Radio. In those lectures he ". . . explore[d] how living in one hemisphere and inheriting our culture from another affected who we are and the sort of world we make for ourselves in Australia".'

¶ Much of Malouf's work, including his prizewinning novel *An Imaginary Life*, an imaginative recreation of Ovid's exile, explores changing cultures in a global world.

NIKI SLADE

Music therapist and trumpeter

Mawlānā Jalāl al-Dīn Rūmī

(1207–73) (AH 604–72)

The Guest House

This being human is a guest house.
Every morning a new arrival.

A joy, a depression, a meanness,
some momentary awareness comes
as an unexpected visitor.

Welcome and entertain them all!
Even if they're a crowd of sorrows,
who violently sweep your house
empty of its furniture,

still, treat each guest honourably.
He may be clearing you out
for some new delight.

The dark thought, the shame, the malice,
meet them at the door laughing,
And invite them in.

Be grateful for whoever comes,
because each has been sent
as a guide from beyond.

'I have always loved the words of Mawlānā Jalāl al-Dīn Rūmī and they
have been a great help to me when in difficulty.'

GWEN SLADE

Former academic economist

Dame Roma Mitchell

(1913–2000)

I suppose generosity of spirit is more important really than anything else.

Dame Roma Mitchell, a remark in a television programme,
Australian Biography II, 4 June 1993, SBS

'Dame Roma Mitchell was the first woman QC in Australia (1962), the
first woman Supreme Court judge, the first woman Chancellor of a
university in Australia (University of Adelaide, 1983–90) and the first
woman governor of an Australian State (of South Australia, 1991–6).
A committed Roman Catholic with a strong sense of natural justice,
she led reform on Aboriginal issues, suffrage, child protection and
human rights.'

PETER G. H. SPEKE

Farmer

Captain John Hanning Speke

(1827–64)

Most beautiful was the scene, nothing could surpass it! It was the very perfection of the kind of effect aimed at in a highly kept park; with a magnificent stream from 600 to 700 yards wide, dotted with islets and rocks, the former occupied by fishermens' huts, the latter by terns and crocodiles basking in the sun, flowing between high grassy banks, with rich trees and plantains in the background, where herds of the n'sunnu and hartebeest could be seen grazing, while the hippopotami were snorting in the water and florican* and Guinea-fowl were rising at our feet.

John Hanning Speke, from *The Journal of the Discovery of the Source of the Nile*

On 3 August 1858, Speke ascended to the top of a long low hill from which he saw for the first time the huge expanse of the Ukerewe Sea,† receding pale and placidly into the far distance. This, for Speke, was the greatest moment of the journey, and perhaps the greatest moment of his life.

Alexander Maitland, from *Speke*

'My great-great-uncle, John Hanning Speke, discovered and named Lake Victoria Nyanza, the source reservoir of the Nile in Central Africa. Captain Speke left England when he was 17 to join the Indian Army. He left India when he was 27 to explore central Africa, and returned to England (Somerset) aged 36 and died when he was only 37.'

¶ *Or 'florikan', a small bustard. †Lake Victoria.

DUNCAN SPROTT

Novelist, Co. Cork

※ ※

An anonymous ancient Egyptian harper

(*c.* 1160 BC)

The Harper's Song for Inherkhawy

I

All who come into being as flesh
pass on, and have since God walked the earth;
and young blood mounts to their places.

II

So seize the day! Hold holiday!
Be unwearied, unceasing, alive,
you and your own true love;
Let not your heart be troubled during your
    sojourn on earth,
but seize the day as it passes!

Put incense and sweet oil upon you,
garlanded flowers at your breast,
While the lady alive in your heart for ever
delights, as she sits beside you.

Grieve not your heart, whatever comes;
let sweet music play before you;
Recall not the evil, loathsome to God,
But have joy, joy, joy and pleasure!

O upright man, man just and true,
patient and kind, content with your lot,
rejoicing, not speaking evil:–
Let your heart be drunk on the gift of Day
until that day comes when you anchor.

Anonymous ancient Egyptian harper

'This ancient Egyptian harper's song, from the tomb of Inherk-hawy, is a nice reminder when you're worrying about what happened last week, or what will happen tomorrow, to think of *today*.'

¶ Inherkhawy was Chief of Workmen in the Place of Truth (the necropolis). He lived during the reigns of Rameses III and Rameses IV and owns Tomb 359 at Deir el-Medineh in western Thebes. Could Horace have known this song when he wrote: *Carpe Diem, quam minimum credula postero* (Seize today, and put as little trust as you can in the morrow).

ANN STEADMAN
Teacher

Linda Headland

(1948–)

Imagine you are starving and presented with a dead elephant: if you had any sense you would not rush to tear out hunks to stuff yourselves with; you would take a knife and cut away a bit at a time. You must do the same with your work, take it a little at a time and be happy with slow progress.

Linda Headland

'Linda Headland is the wonderful, modest director of Elcap. She had the vision to foresee as feasible a better life for those shut away in asylums or institutions, and the determination to see it through in only 20 years. She is a superb manager and inspirer of her workforce, each of whom she knows personally, as she does all 100 of those in her care. She has advised on the development of Mental Health Acts, and Elcap is a flagship of excellence for other organizations.'

¶ Elcap cares for the severely disabled and wheelchair bound in East Lothian. The life of Ann's daughter Nell, who has extreme disabilities, 'has been transformed by Elcap's care and she now has a wondrous quality of life'.

DR DAVID STEVENS

Leader of the Corrymeela Community, Northern Ireland

Revd Dr Ray Davey

(1915–)

> If we Christians cannot speak the message of reconciliation, we
> have nothing to say.
>
> Revd Dr Ray Davey

'The Revd Dr Ray Davey worked for the YMCA and was a prisoner of
war in Germany just outside Dresden when it was firebombed. Later,
when Presbyterian chaplain at Queen's University Belfast he, with a
group of students and former students, founded the Corrymeela
Community in 1965 on the beautiful windswept Antrim coast. He
foresaw the need for a centre of reconciliation and rest, well before
open hostilities broke out between the divided communities in
Northern Ireland in 1969. Ray retired in 1980 but his work carries
on.'

¶ Corrymeela means Hill of Harmony and the centre lives up to its name by
providing the context for friendship, reconciliation and conflict resolution on
local and international fronts. Much of the work is done by young volunteers
from around the world, and over the years Corrymeela has been a beacon of
hope to many.

Groups may come for a week or just a weekend. Sometimes it might be a
group of children from mixed backgrounds; sometimes a group of families with
disabled children; or adults from mixed faiths or troubled backgrounds needing
to find common ground.

Corrymeela has its own brand of Northern Irish humour. Here, for instance,
you can discover that there are subtle differences between 'Catholic tea' and
'Protestant tea' depending on whether a mouse could run over it without
drowning, the quantity of tannin, sugar, milk or undrinkableness. Such are the
nuances that can divide us – and we haven't even considered the temperature
and order of the ingredients.

Lawrence of Arabia

(1888–1935)

All men dream: but not equally. Those who dream by night in the dusty recesses of their minds wake in the day to find that it was vanity: but the dreamers of the day are dangerous men, for they may act their dream with open eyes, to make it possible.

T. E. Lawrence, from *The Seven Pillars of Wisdom*

'I have been inspired by many quotes and the lives of many people throughout history. This quote hangs framed on my office wall. I suppose some would question his use of the word "dangerous", but it doesn't bother me. I am moved by the distinctions between "day-dreaming" and being a "dreamer of the day", and all the implications for one's focus, actions and conduct that these convey.'

¶ Kathy Sullivan also sent the following quotation and comment:

> Les meilleures idées ne sont pas celles que l'on a,
> Ni même celles que l'on donne,
> Mais celles que l'on suscite.

> The best ideas are not the ones you've got,
> Nor even the ones you give,
> But the ones you stir up.
> > Michel Godet (1948–)

She said: 'I often sense or glimpse very vaguely things I know are important long before I can describe them or express them sufficiently to pass muster with conventional judges!'

Dr Kathryn Sullivan was the first woman to walk in space. She is a veteran of three shuttle missions, and has logged over 532 hours in space. The combination of her deep-sea diving and space missions leaves her as the woman who has travelled more vertical miles than any other.

Professor Michel Godet is a scientist, economist and mathematician.

DOM ANTONY SUTCH

Parish priest, Beccles

Daniel of Beccles

(*c.* twelfth century)

If the wife of your lord turns her eyes too often and wantonly looses shameful fires against you, letting you know that she wants to have intercourse with you; if she says, 'The whole household and your lord, my husband, shall serve you for ever, you alone shall be my darling, you shall rule everything, everything which belongs to your lord shall be open to you', . . . consult me my son: what I counsel is planted in your heart; between two evils, choose the lesser evil; your safer plan is to feign illness, nerve-racking diseases, to go away sensibly and prudently.

Daniel of Beccles

'Daniel of Beccles was known as the author of *Urbunas Magnus* or 'The Book of the Civilised Man', a 3,000-line Latin poem. He was probably a courtier, living in the late twelfth century; and may have been a monk or a teacher. I'm just delighted by this piece, which is written as a poem; by the fact that he is amusing and sensible and full of wisdom; and is from the town where I am parish priest.'

St Benedict

(*c.* 480–*c.* 550)

Let him (the Abbot) be prudent and considerate in all his commands; and whether the work which he enjoins concern God or the world, let him always be discreet and moderate, bearing in mind the discretion of holy Jacob who said: 'If I cause my flocks to be over-driven, they will all perish in one day.' So imitating these and others examples of discretion, the mother of the virtues, let him so temper

all things that the strong may still have something to strive after and
the bruised need not be broken.

St Benedict, *The Rule of St Benedict*, chapter 64,
translated by Abbot Justin McCann, 1952

'The longer I have been a Benedictine monk, the more I have come to
appreciate St Benedict's humanity. His Rule for monks is wise and
compassionate. He truly aims to bring people gently to God. He has
had a considerable influence in Europe and the world. His Rule is
everywhere, even adapted for the laity.'

PETER THOMAS SWAN

Retired company director

The Revd Augustus Toplady

(1740–78)

Rock of Ages

Rock of ages, cleft to me,
Let me hide myself in thee;
Let the water and the blood,
From thy riven side which flowed,
Be of sin and double cure:
Cleanse me from its guilt and power.

While I draw this fleeting breath,
When mine eyes are closed in death,
When I soar through tracts unknown,
See thee on thy judgment throne;
Rock of ages, cleft to me,
Let me hide myself in thee.

Augustus Toplady

'These verses were written in 1775 by Toplady, vicar of a small parish in Devon, shortly after being caught in a thunderstorm while walking and taking shelter under an overhanging rock. For me, his words express how helpless we are, and how we look for total love and forgiveness from our Saviour.'

JILL SYKES

Nonagenarian, dog-lover and former Land Girl

George Herbert Hirst

(1871–1954)

What can you have better than a nice green field, with the wickets set up, and to go out and do the best for your side?

George Hirst at Scarborough on his last day of first-class cricket, September 1921

'George Hirst was already a legend as the finest cricketer since W. G. Grace by the time I started watching cricket. It wasn't just his superb cricket (and he still holds the record for taking 200 wickets and making over 2,000 runs for the greatest number of first-class cricket seasons), it was also his reputation for modesty, kindness and good humour which engendered such affection. The crowd would be willing him to achieve his goals. It is said that on one occasion, as he approached a 200th wicket, two elderly ladies, one Hirst's mother, were so overcome that they stayed walking outside the ground, beyond the break for the tea interval. Nothing changes much.'

PHIL SYKES

Plastic surgeon

Henry de Mondeville

(1260–1320)

No craftsman should work on an object without knowing it. Being the human body the object of the whole medical art, of which surgery is one of the instruments, it is obvious that a surgeon who practises incisions on the different areas of the body and on its limbs without being aware of their anatomy will never operate well.

Henry de Mondeville, from *Chirugie*

'Henry de Mondeville, Surgeon to Philippe le Bel and his son Louis X of France, is one of my surgical heroes. His name crops up repeatedly in the early history of surgery. This quote is taken from the beginning of his work *Chirugie*, written over 700 years ago. It is self-evident and simple. But in the modern world of hi-tech medicine and surgery, it can so easily be overlooked. The increasing demand for time in the medical curriculum means that a valuable study of anatomy has become limited. Though specialized surgeons may only need to know about *their own anatomical area* in detail, it is sad that the study of a fascinating subject is at risk.'

TSERING TASHI

Representative of H.H. the Dalai Lama, Office of Tibet, London

His Holiness the Dalai Lama

(1935–)

As a Buddhist monk, my concern extends to all members of the human family and, indeed, to all sentient beings who suffer. I believe all suffering is caused by ignorance. People inflict pain on others in the selfish pursuit of their happiness or satisfaction.

Yet true happiness comes from a sense of brotherhood and sisterhood. We need to cultivate a universal responsibility for one another and the planet we share. Although I have found my own Buddhist religion helpful in generating love and compassion, even for those we consider our enemies, I am convinced that everyone can develop a good heart and a sense of universal responsibility, with or without religion.

The Dalai Lama, from his Nobel Peace Prize acceptance speech, 10 December 1989

'His Holiness the Dalai Lama, the spiritual and temporal leader of the Tibetan people, has inspired me in many ways, through his actions and words of wisdom, such as not having hatred even to those who have perpetrated suffering. It is following the advice of His Holiness that I have met many Chinese scholars and students both in the United States and in the UK, and learned that some of the Chinese people can become supportive of the just cause of Tibet after hearing the Tibetan experience of suffering under the authoritarian Chinese rule.'

JULIAN TEMPERLEY

Cider brandy maker, Somerset

Giocante Casabianca

(1786?–98)

Casabianca

The boy stood on the burning deck
Whence all but he had fled;
The flame that lit the battle's wreck
Shone round him o'er the dead.

Yet beautiful and bright he stood,
As born to rule the storm;
A creature of heroic blood,
A proud, though child-like form.

The flames rolled on – he would not go
Without his Father's word;
That father, faint in death below,
His voice no longer heard.

He called aloud – 'Say, father, say
If yet my task is done?'
He knew not that the chieftain lay
Unconscious of his son.

'Speak, father!' once again he cried,
'If I may yet be gone!'
And but the booming shots replied,
And fast the flames rolled on.

Upon his brow he felt their breath,
And in his waving hair,
And looked from that lone post of death
In still yet brave despair.

And shouted but once more aloud,
'My father! must I stay?'
While o'er him fast, through sail and shroud,
The wreathing fires made way.

They wrapt the ship in splendour wild,
They caught the flag on high,
And streamed above the gallant child,
Like banners in the sky.

There came a burst of thunder sound –
The boy – oh! Where was he?
Ask of the winds that far around
With fragments strewed the sea! –

With mast, and helm, and pennon fair,
That well had borne their part –
But the noblest thing which perished there
Was that young faithful heart.

Felicia Hemans (1793–1835)

'I have loved this poem since I was a boy. It is true heroism.'

¶ The poem commemorates an incident that occurred in 1798 during the Battle of the Nile on board the French ship *L'Orient*. Giocante, the son of Captain Louis de Casabianca, remained at his post and perished when the flames caused the magazine to explode. He was about 12 years old.

Sir Crispin Tickell

Diplomat and retired ambassador

Hildegard of Bingen

(1098–1179)

I, the fiery life of divine wisdom,
I ignite the beauty of the plains,
I sparkle the waters,
I burn in the sun, and the moon, and the stars,
With wisdom I order all rightly . . .
I adorn all the Earth,
I am the breeze that nurtures all things green . . .
I am the rain coming from the dew that causes
    the grasses to laugh with
the joy of life.
I call forth tears, the aroma of holy work.
I am the yearning for good.

Hildegard of Bingen

'The thought behind this underlies all religion and respect for life on Earth.'

¶ Hildegard of Bingen was also chosen by the Hon. Sir Jonathon Porritt, environmentalist, former Director of Friends of the Earth; and Dr Desmond Graves, retired management teacher.

CHARLES TINDAL

Farmer and creamery director, Co. Donegal

≈

Horatio, Viscount Nelson

(1758–1805)

Time is everything. Five minutes makes the difference between victory and defeat.

Horatio, Viscount Nelson

'I have always felt that so much of life depends on whether we do what we should now, rather than later, which is really the same as not doing it at all!'

MILLIE CATH

Age 11, North Cadbury Church of England Primary School, Somerset

≈

Johnny's Tiger

Johnny made a tiger in the sandpit miss,
He said it really bites miss,
Mary hurt her finger miss,
She said it hurted when she poked
Johnny's tiger miss,
It's so big and fierce miss,
That no-one's in the sandpit anymore miss!
Johnny's tiger has got huge eyes miss,
And teeth are so sharp!
'Johnny! What is this all about a biting tiger?'
'It really bites miss! Ask Mary.'
'I wouldn't knock it down miss,
It'll eat you.'

Gulp!

Johnny's tiger ate miss, sir!
It hurted Mary's finger sir,
But I wouldn't knock it down sir . . .

Millie Cath

RICHARD TODD
Actor

Bernard, Viscount Montgomery of Alamein
(1887–1976)

Therefore, let every officer and man enter the battle with a stout heart, and the determination to do his duty so long as he has breath in his body.

Bernard, Viscount Montgomery of Alamein, from Montgomery's
personal message to all troops of the Eighth Army, before the
Battle of El Alamein, 23 October 1942

'I have particular admiration for Bernard, Viscount Montgomery of Alamein, and he is memorable to me as a hero and saviour because I served in his XII Corps soon after Dunkirk, and began to realize the effect that his determination and military skills had on the beleaguered and demoralized British Army. He is mainly famed for his command of our British and American forces leading to the cessation of the war in Europe, and as the saviour of the British way of life.

One day he visited the dug-out in Normandy where I, as a young man, had set up my information centre. He predicted that we would be in Brussels in ten days. This seemed an impossible task, but he was right.'

LADY XA TOLLEMACHE

Landscape and garden designer

St Francis of Assisi

(1181–1226)

Start by doing what's necessary; then do what's possible; and suddenly you are doing the impossible.

St Francis of Assisi

'Being a gardener and lover of animals, St Francis inspired me because he blended the spirituality of life and its connection to the environment and all wildlife. He reached out to the sick and was acutely aware of all disadvantaged people. He also accepted the important role of women! At present, with the environment so fragile, we need him back.'

¶ This quotation, usually attributed to St Francis, appears on numerous websites, but the Editor could not find any primary source.

SUSAN TOMES

Classical musician and writer

Shoji Hamada

(1894–1978)

If a kiln is small, I might be able to control it completely, that is to say, my own self can become a controller, a master of the kiln. But man's own self is but a small thing after all. When I work at the large kiln, the power of my own self becomes so feeble that it cannot control it adequately. It means that for the large kiln, the power that is beyond me is necessary. Without the mercy of such invisible power I cannot get good pieces. One of the reasons I wanted to have a large kiln is because I want to be a potter, if I may, who works more in grace than in his own power. You know, nearly all of the best old pots were done in huge kilns.

Shoji Hamada, quoted in Becoming Bamboo Western and Eastern
Exploration of the Meaning of Life, by Robert Edgar Carter

'I have always enjoyed looking at and using hand-made pottery. This quote, from the Japanese potter Shoji Hamada, means a lot to me. Although Hamada speaks of the art of pottery, his words also have a much wider spiritual resonance. As a musician, I have found them inspiring when preparing music for performance.'

¶ Shoji Hamada, one of the great Japanese potters, produced simple stoneware pots with ash or iron glazes and abstract brushwork designs. In 1920 he came to England and helped Bernard Leach, who had worked with him in Japan, to set up the Leach pottery studio in St Ives. This had a major influence on British pottery.

FIONA TORRENS-SPENCE

Army camp follower and author

❧

Edith Cavell

(1865–1915)

I am thankful to have had these ten weeks of quiet to get ready. Now I have had them and have been kindly treated here. I expected my sentence and I believe it was just. Standing as I do in view of God and Eternity I realize patriotism is not enough. I must have no hatred or bitterness towards anyone.

Edith Cavell, words spoken by her to the German Lutheran
Prison Chaplain on 10 October 1915, the eve of her execution by a firing squad

'Living in a world where it is all too easy to hate people from other races or religions, I admire Edith Cavell's Christian view. Cavell, who was also my Australian grandmother's heroine, began nursing for the princely sum of £10 per annum at a time when nursing was not considered a suitable career for young ladies. She put her life at risk helping in slum areas, particularly during a typhoid epidemic, and was instrumental in setting up a training school and raising regard for nursing. Had it not been for the war, she might have remained an unsung spinster of the Victorian era. A woman imbued with Christian values, and with complete disregard for self, she is best known for the heroic way in which she helped British servicemen escape from behind enemy lines in Belgium, and for which she was executed.'

¶ These words of Edith Cavell's were also chosen by PROFESSOR LORD LAYARD OF HIGHGATE, economist.

Edith Cavell's statue is near St Martin-in-the-Fields London.

WILLIAM TREVOR

Writer

Honore de Balzac

(1799–1850)

It is as absurd to say that a man can't love one woman all the time as it is to say that a violinist needs several violins to play the same piece of music.

Honore de Balzac

'This is an observation of Balzac's that I particularly delight in.'

SIR MARK TULLY

Writer and broadcaster

Rabindranath Tagore

(1861–1941)

In ancient India we find that the circumstances of forest life did not overcome man's minds, and did not enfeeble the current of his energies, but only gave to it a particular direction . . . His aim was not to enquire but to realise, to enlarge his consciousness by growing with and growing into his surroundings . . . To realize this great harmony between man's spirit and the spirit of the world was the endeavour of the forest dwellers of ancient India . . .

The West seems to take pride in thinking that it is subduing nature; as if we are living in a hostile world where we have to wrest everything we want from an unwilling and alien arrangement of things.

Rabindranath Tagore, extracts from the *Sadhana Essays*

'Rabindranath Tagore was a polymath, one of the most renowned figures of the Indian Renaissance and much admired by Mahatma Gandhi. He was a poet, musician, artist and writer. I admire him because his writings embody the essential spirit of India which I believe is so relevant to the world today.'

THE MOST REVD DESMOND MPILO TUTU

Anglican Archbishop Emeritus of Cape Town

St Francis of Assisi

(1181–1226)

O Lord, make me an instrument of Thy Peace!
Where there is hatred, let me sow love;
Where there is injury, pardon;
Where there is discord, harmony;

Where there is doubt, faith;
Where there is despair, hope;
Where there is darkness, light, and
Where there is sorrow, joy.
Oh Divine Master, grant that I may not
so much seek to be consoled as to console;
to be understood as to understand; to be loved
as to love; for it is in giving that we receive;
It is in pardoning that we are pardoned;
and it is in dying that we are born to Eternal Life.

St Francis of Assisi

¶ This prayer was also chosen by ALICE BASIL SAHHAR, founder and director of Jeel Al Amal Home for Children in East Jerusalem. The Home is a Christian foundation but takes children of any creed or nationality. Alice says: 'In what language does a baby cry?'

The prayer was a favourite of Mother Teresa of Calcutta and is sometimes ascribed to her rather than to St Francis, but it is commonly known as St Francis' Prayer.

SOFIA BAGLIETTO

Age 8, Lorretto Convent Junior School, Gibraltar

St Francis of Assisi

St Francis came from a town called Assisi,
His childhood was very comfy and easy.

When he grew up he gave up all he had,
His rich father thought he was mad.

He lived like a beggar, his clothes always brown,
He liked the woods but not the town.

He spoke to the animals and looked after the poor.
And when he died, he was made a Saint for sure.

Sofia Baglietto

RUSSELL TWISK

Former editor-in-chief of *Reader's Digest*

George Herbert

(1593–1633)

But as I raved and grew more fierce and wild
At every word,
Methought I heard one calling, Child!
And I replied, My Lord.

George Herbert, last lines from 'The Collar'

'George Herbert, the poet-priest, is a constant inspiration to me. He was a highly educated man, followed an academic career at Cambridge, and could have easily attained high political office. Instead he listened to that still, small voice, took holy orders in 1630 and spent the last three years of his life as rector of the tiny church, St Andrew's at Bemerton, near Salisbury. Here he wrote hymns and poems which were not published until after his death from consumption just before his fortieth birthday. His hymns are still sung all over the world.'

JOHN TYDEMAN

Retired Head of BBC Radio Drama

John Donne

(1572–1631)

No man is an island entire of itself; every man is a piece of the continent, a part of the main . . . Any man's death diminishes me, because I am involved in mankind. And therefore never send to know for whom the bell tolls: it tolls for thee.

John Donne, from *Devotions*, Meditation 17

'As a schoolboy I thought I was very special in alone discovering the poetry of John Donne, a contemporary of Shakespeare, and as good a poet – which indeed he is. I had been brought up to believe that no man was an island, and I knew the expression 'For whom the bell tolls' as the title of an Ernest Hemingway novel and film. It was much later that I learned that both dictums were linked and were from the prose work of *my* John Donne.'

❡ John Donne was also chosen by MORAR LUCAS, voluntary worker, who chose this sonnet from *Divine Meditations*:

> At the round earth's imagined corners, blow
> Your trumpets, angels, and arise, arise
> From death, you numberless infinities
> Of souls, and to your scattered bodies go,
> All whom the flood did, and fire shall o'erthrow,
> All whom war, dearth, age, agues, tyrannies,
> Despair, law, chance, hath slain, and you whose eyes,
> Shall behold God, and never taste death's woe.
> But let them sleep, Lord, and me mourn a space,
> For, if above all these, my sins abound,
> 'Tis late to ask abundance of thy grace,
> When we are there; here on this lowly ground,
> Teach me how to repent; for that's as good
> As if thou hadst sealed my pardon, with thy blood.

SARAH VAUGHAN

General Practitioner

Ffyona Campbell

(1967–)

'Ffyona Campbell started her walk when she was 16, walking from John O'Groats to Land's End, and over the next 11 years she did one cross-continental walk after another, building up to the official criterion for a walk round the world (this has to cross four continents and end in the place it began). She would have been the first woman to walk round the world, and would have made it into the *Guinness Book of*

Records. However, on her first cross-continental walk at the age of 18 she accepted lifts for a part of the walk. Although nobody else found out, she felt unable to bear taking credit for something she knew she hadn't really done. She went back to the USA, completed the part of the walk she hadn't done properly before, and then admitted publicly to what she'd done and rescinded her right to the title of first woman to walk round the world. Without that, it would have been just another success-against-the-odds story, but it made me realize something important – what indicates our character is not just our successes, but how we respond to our failures.'

STEPHEN VENABLES

First mountaineer to ascend Everest without oxygen

Eric Shipton

(1907–77)

There are few treasures of more lasting worth than the experiences of a way of life that is in itself wholly satisfying. Such, after all, are the only possessions of which no fate, no cosmic catastrophe can deprive us; nothing can alter the fact if for one moment in eternity we have really lived.

Eric Shipton, closing words from *Upon That Mountain –*
The Six Mountain Travel Books

'Eric Shipton, who took five expeditions to Everest, was one of the greatest explorers of the twentieth century. He wrote these words in 1943 when the future of the western world, let alone of any climbing possibilities, was uncertain. In 1939 he had been camping on the upper Biafo Glacier at the heart of the Karakoram range, hoping to explore even more remote areas, when news of the war reached him. The expedition was abandoned and all hopes were dashed.'

¶ In 1939 Eric Shipton wrote this description: 'The cliffs and ridges of K2 rose out of the glacier in one stupendous sweep to the summit of the mountain, 12,000 feet above. The sight was beyond my comprehension, and I sat gazing at it, with a kind of timid fascination, watching wreaths of mist creep in and out of corries, utterly remote. I saw ice avalanches, weighing perhaps hundreds of tons, break off from a hanging glacier, nearly two miles above my head; the ice was ground to a fine powder and drifted away in the breeze long before it reached the foot of the precipice, nor did any sound reach my ears ... It was an hour before Tilman returned and we hurried back down the glacier, for it was late in the afternoon and we had a long way to go. By the time we reached Ila, the weather had made a sudden change for the worse. Great billows of cloud were rolling over the peaks from the south and a cold blustering wind blew up the glacier. Before every thing was blotted out we were able to erect the theodolite ...' (Eric Shipton, from *Blank on the Map – The Six Mountain Travel Books.*)

MAJOR GENERAL CHARLES VYVYAN

Former army officer; now working in the City and Wall Street

❧ ❧

Edward the Black Prince*

(1330–76)

You who pass silently by here where this body rests, listen to what I would say to you if I were able to speak. Such as you are, I used to be; you will become such as I am. I did not ponder on the idea of death whilst I was alive. On Earth I possessed great wealth with which I kept high estate: lands, houses, and great treasure, rich furnishings, horses, silver, and gold. But now I am poor and wretched as I lie here in the dust. All my fine apparel is gone, my flesh is quite decayed. I inhabit a meagre and narrow house. You would not credit that it is I if you were to see me now. You would fancy that this could never have been any man, so utterly changed am I. For God's good sake, pray to the King of Heaven that He may have mercy on my soul. All those who, on my account, pray that God may receive me, may God take them to His paradise where wicked persons may not be.

Inscription in Norman-French around the Black Prince's tomb
in Canterbury Cathedral

'Edward, the son of Edward III, won his spurs, the famous ostrich plumes and the motto *Homout: ich Dene*† (or *Dien*) at the battle of

Crecy, 26 August 1346. An original Knight of the Garter, he played a significant part in the defeat of the French at the Battle of Poitiers on 19 September 1356 and afterwards treated the French King John II with great courtesy. He ruled as the Prince of Aquitaine, but despite another victory at Najéra, his reign was an administrative failure, and having contracted an illness while on an offensive military operation in Spain, he returned to England in 1371 as a sick and broken man.

Despite all this, the Black Prince embodied the growing concern for a more chivalrous world, which was to find its purest expression 100 years later in Malory's "Morte d'Arthur". His epitaph reflects the spiritual dimension and the humility associated with it.'

¶ *The epithet is said to come from the colour of his battle armour.
†Courage; I serve (as spelled by Edward himself).

THE RT HON. LORD WADDINGTON

Former Governor of Bermuda

Sir Winston Churchill

(1874–1965)

Which way shall we turn to save our lives and the future of the World? It does not matter so much to older people, they are going soon anyway. But I find it poignant to look at youth with all its activity and ardour, and wonder what would lie before them if God wearied of mankind.

Winston Churchill

'This is an extract from Winston Churchill's last speech in the House of Commons. I find it very moving. Churchill was not noted for his religious convictions, but in the evening of his life and after he had saved his country and helped rescue Europe from Nazi tyranny, the world was facing the new threat of nuclear annihilation, and in this passage Churchill seems almost tormented by the thought that all he had done might prove to have been in vain. John Dryden had alternative thoughts about this.'

Happy the man and happy he alone
He who today can call his own;
He, who secure within, can say
Tomorrow do thy worst, for I have lived today.
Be fair, or foul, or rain or shine,
The joys I have possessed, in spite of fate, are mine.
Not Heaven itself upon the past has power.
But what has been, has been, and I have had my hour.

John Dryden (1631–1700)

'This is a beautiful passage which should give comfort to anyone who, having tried to do his best, is facing difficulties, hardship or grief.'

Sir Robert Wade-Gery
Former High Commissioner to India

Sydney Smith
(1771–1845)

I am just going to pray for you at St Paul's, but with no very lively hope of success.

Sydney Smith

'The Revd Sydney Smith, Canon of St Paul's and genial wit, was also the author of the charming poem 'Recipe for Salad' which includes the well-known lines:

> Serenely full, the epicure would say,
> Fate cannot harm me, I have dined today.'

HRH The Prince of Wales

❧

Cicero

(106–43 BC)

To be ignorant of what occurred before you were born is to remain always a child, for what is the worth of a human life unless it is woven into the lives of our ancestors by the records of history?

Cicero, from *Orator ad M. Brutum*, Chapter 34, Section 120,
a speech dedicated to Brutus

¶ Cicero – lawyer, prolific writer, philosopher, politician and orator – was a giant of the later years of the Roman Republic. Of his oratory, Quintilian said that 'his name was synonymous with oratory', and the historian Livy that 'a second Cicero would be needed to praise him adequately'. In philosophy we owe him such words as 'appetite', 'comprehension', 'definition', 'difference', 'element', 'individual', 'induction', 'infinity', 'moral property', and 'notion'. He gave us the precept of asking, when faced with a problem of crime, '*Quis, cui, quando, quomodo, cui bono*' ('Who did it, to whom, when, how and to who's advantage?'). Sometimes writing as an agnostic, sometimes as a theist, in Scipio's dream at the end of *De republica* he gives us a sublime vision of a future life.

Petrarch said of him, 'You could sometimes fancy it is not a pagan philosopher, but a Christian apostle who is speaking', and Voltaire that 'we honour Cicero who taught us how to think'. Julias Caesar, his great adversary, gave him the accolade that 'it is better to have extended the frontiers of the mind than to have pushed back the boundaries of empire' (Pliny, *Naturalis Historia*, 7, 31).

Sir Harold Walker

Former Ambassador to Iraq

❧

Admiral Lord Nelson

(1758–1805)

May the Great God, whom I worship, grant to my Country and for the benefit of Europe in general a great and glorious victory; and

---

may no misconduct in anyone tarnish it; and may humanity after
Victory be the predominant feature of the British Fleet.

Admiral the Lord Nelson, a diary entry on the eve of the
Battle of Trafalgar, 21 October 1805

'Admiral Lord Nelson was no saint: he let his wife down; he was vain.
But he had attributes that made him both a leader and a hero: apart
from his faith, he had an outstanding sense of duty and he cared for
the men under him.'

SIR PETER WALLIS

Retired diplomat

Gamaliel

(First century)

Refrain from these men, and let them alone: for if this counsel or
this work be of men, it will come to nought: but if it be of God, ye
cannot overthrow it; lest haply ye be found even to fight against
God.

Acts 5.38–39 (AV)

'I have always admired Gamaliel, for his courage in standing up to his
colleagues and his wisdom in seeing that human activities have their
own momentum and that interventions can have unintended consequences. His philosophy chimes with a view widely held in the
Diplomatic Service that the right thing to do is often nothing; but
that can be a difficult and unpopular position to adopt, as Gamaliel
found.'

❡ Gamaliel was the first of a line of six sages of that name. This was the advice
he gave to the Council in Jerusalem, who were planning to kill Peter and other
apostles because of their preaching. Gamaliel is also known as the teacher of St
Paul, and for his decision to allow a woman to remarry on the evidence of a
single witness to her husband's death.

THE RT HON. THE LADY WARNOCK

House of Lords cross-bencher, philosopher,
Chairman of the Committee of Inquiry on Human Fertilization

❦

Matthew Arnold

(1822–88)

Dover Beach

. . . The Sea of Faith
Was once, too, at the full, and round earth's shore
Lay like the folds of a bright girdle furl'd;
But now I only hear
Its melancholy, long, withdrawing roar,
Retreating to the breath
Of the night-wind, down the vast edges drear
And naked shingles of the world . . .

Ah, love, let us be true
To one another! for the world, which seems
To lie before us like a land of dreams,
So various, so beautiful, so new,
Hath really neither joy, nor love, nor light,
Nor certitude, nor peace, nor help for pain;
And we are here as on a darkling plain
Swept with confused alarms of struggle and flight,
Where ignorant armies clash by night.

Matthew Arnold, from *Poems*, 1885

'I think most of the people I admire are writers or musicians, because one can come back to them again and again and find more in what they have done. But it's difficult to illustrate musicians in a book. So that leaves writers. In the end, after thinking about Aristotle, who is one of my greatest heroes, I chose instead Matthew Arnold. He was a great thinker and critic and sometimes a great poet. But what I mostly admire and love is that he was so much torn by the battle between the new Darwinian theories and the old acceptance of

Christianity that he felt it to the heart and couldn't bear it . . . all comfort withdrawn. But throughout, he kept his deep imaginative sense of eternity all around him. 'Dover Beach' is especially relevant to us now, it seems to me.'

PAULINE M. WEBB

Writer and broadcaster

☙ ❧

Martin Luther King Jr

(1929–68)

To our most bitter opponents we say: 'We shall match your capacity to inflict suffering by our capacity to endure suffering. We shall meet your physical force with our soul force. Do to us what you will and we shall continue to love you. We cannot in all good conscience obey your unjust laws, because non-co-operation with evil is as much a moral obligation as is co-operation with good. Throw us in jail and we shall still love you. Send your hooded perpetrators of violence into our community at the midnight hour and beat us and leave us half dead, and we shall still love you. But be ye assured that we will wear you down by our capacity to suffer. One day we shall win freedom, but not only for ourselves. We shall so appeal to your heart and conscience that we shall win you in the process, and our victory will be a double victory.'

Martin Luther King Jr, from *Strength to Love*, 1963

'I have chosen as my hero and saint, the Revd Martin Luther King Jr, prophet and leader of the Civil Rights Campaign in the USA. Living in New York at the time of his campaign, I was inspired particularly by the sermons he preached on the subject of the love that motivated his whole life. I subsequently became totally committed to the Programme to Combat Racism, launched by the World Council of Churches shortly after he was assassinated, and throughout all the controversy caused by that programme I continued to be inspired by what Martin Luther King had taught us about the strength of love.'

Thomas Donne

Aged 10, Ash School, Somerset

Bobby Charlton

(1937–)

Playing football for his country,
Scoring his team to success.
Surviving disaster,
Being fair and still determined.
Lifting the world cup in glory
And bringing hope to all his fans.

Thomas Donne

Major General Sir Evelyn Webb-Carter

Retired army officer and Controller of the Army Benevolent Fund

Field Marshal Viscount Slim

(1891–1970)

As a soldier I have been asked to say something about the greatest soldier I have met and known. So I am going to. The funny thing is, I can't tell you his name. It changes. Sometimes he has got an English name, sometimes Scottish, sometimes Welsh or Irish. That's because the soldier I want to talk about, the greatest soldier I have met, and believe me, I have met a lot of all sorts, is the *ordinary British soldier.*

Field Marshal Viscount Slim, BBC broadcast, May 1951

'This quotation echoes my feelings exactly, and I think this is rather appropriate at this time.'

UNKNOWN SOLDIER

Sir Arnold Wesker
Playwright

Della, my sister

Father, hear the prayer we offer:
Not for ease that prayer shall be,
But for strength that we may ever
Live our lives courageously.

From a poem by Love Maria Willis (1824–1908)

'We have in Yiddish the word "*mensch*". Literally it means "man" but it has come to mean someone of integrity, honesty and reliability – a sweet and strong personality. It can be applied to both sexes.

My sister is both a *mensch* and heroine. She was a sturdy, hardworking and very beautiful woman, married with three children. She fell and broke a knee, which led to other complications. Arthritis rendered dressing a hardship. She developed a tumour behind her left eye, which then had to be removed. And she is now partially deaf. The decline from strength and beauty to disablement and disfigurement was a horrendous process to endure. Her manner of enduring makes her for me heroic.

Had it been me I would have given up. Not Della. She wanted to remain in the world and fulfil her duties. She learned to use a computer, and insisted we be patient with her deafness so that she could participate in family life. She forced herself to continue cooking, religiously conducted her regime of exercises so that her body functioned at the highest possible level.

And through it all she has not complained or made the lives of those around her miserable. She laughs at jokes, struggles with *The Times* crossword, and we play Scrabble when I visit. Together with her supportive, adoring husband Ralph, we three have long discussions about the human condition and the state of the world. Her endurance makes the world endurable. The thought of her lifts me in dark hours.

I asked her what keeps her going. She remembered an American hymn that her music teacher had arranged for organ in the form of a Bach chorale. The arrangement thrilled her, and the words have stayed with her for life.'

TIMOTHY WEST

Actor

Kahlil Gibran

(1883–1931)

There is an old Arabic song that begins, 'Only God and I know what is in my heart.' We all want the little light in us to be taken from under the bushel. The first poet must have suffered much when the cave dwellers laughed at his mad words. He would have given his bow and arrows, everything he possessed, just to have his fellow men know the delight, and the passion which the sunset had created in his soul. It is surely a noble thing to say 'art for art's sake', but is it not nobler to open the eyes of the blind so that they may share the silent joy of your days and nights?

Kahlil Gibran, from a letter sent to Mary Heskell, November 1911

'I'm choosing this excerpt that I value, perhaps more than the person I'm quoting. But "The Prophet" is undoubtedly a major work of spiritual value.'

HARVEY WHITE

Surgeon with interest in medical history

Sir William Osler

(1849–1919)

To study the phenomenon of disease without books is to sail an uncharted sea, while to study books without patients is not to go to sea at all.

Sir William Osler

'William Osler was an outstanding diagnostician, clinician and teacher. His book, *The Principles and Practice of Medicine*, published in 1892, remained an important text for several decades and is still regarded as a classic. I was steeped in Osler as an undergraduate, and there is a lot in it of relevance for students today, if they bothered to read it.'

¶ William Osler was also chosen by DR LUCY JOHNSON.

MARY WHITELEY
Architectural historian

·ᴥ· ᴥ·

King Charles V of France
(1338–80)

O quel tres grant ordonnance en toutes choses! Quel pontificalte! Quel sens! Quel gouvernement! Quel representacion de prince! Quel faconde! Quelle eloquence!

O what a high sense of order in every matter! What priestly dignity! What judgement! What powers of government! What princely example! What fluency! What eloquence!

Christine de Pizan (1365–c. 1440), from *Le Livre de Paix*, 1 fol. 20

'My hero is Charles V, a late-medieval king of France. At the age of 18 all the odds had been against him. His father, John the Good, had been captured by the Black Prince at the Battle of Poitiers, and was being held prisoner in London, with demands for a crippling ransom. Large tracts of France were in English hands, Paris was in revolt, and he himself, a sickly youth who lacked the qualities of the ideal medieval knight, was mistrusted by his father.

However, by the end of his reign, Charles V had successfully brought about the country's recovery, not by military conquest but by his methods of monarchy. So admired were these methods that in 1404 his brother, the Duke of Burgundy, commissioned Christine de Pizan, the well-known author and daughter of the king's doctor, to write his biography. In her book *Le Livre des Fais et Bonnes Meurs du Sage Roy Charles V* she describes the splendour of his daily Court thronged by visitors from all over France and from abroad; the creation of magnificent castles to provide a suitably royal setting; his patronage of literature and the visual arts to help restore the monarchy's prestige; and the way he could be directly approached by both the poorest as well as the most important of his subjects.'

❡ The Black Prince, so successful at Poitiers, bears a marked contrast to Charles V. See entry of CHARLES VYVYAN.

RICHARD WILDING

Retired civil servant

❧ ❧

Robert Browning

(1812–89)

Bishop Blougram's Apology

And now what are we? Unbelievers both,
Calm and complete, determinately fixed
To-day, to-morrow, and forever, pray?
You'll guarantee me that? Not so, I think! ...

Just when we are safest, there's a sunset-touch,
A fancy from a flower-bell, some one's death,
A chorus-ending from Euripides, –
And that's enough for fifty hopes and fears ...

The grand Perhaps! ...

Once feel about, and soon or late you hit
Some sense, in which it might be, after all.
Why not, 'The Way, the Truth, the Life?'

Lines 173–97 of 'Bishop Blougram's Apology' from
Poetical Works 1888–1894

'My favourite doubter, Robert Browning, was no saint. But his series "Men and Women" represents for me a heroic mental struggle between belief and disbelief – a collection of private interviews with a God who may or may not be there (the great Perhaps). In this poem, the Bishop challenges Mr Gigadibs the journalist: "Let's assume that we both abandon all belief." The passage quoted seems to me to challenge everybody.'

FRANK WILLIAMS

Actor (the Vicar in *Dad's Army*)

William Shakespeare

(1564–1616)

There is a tide in the affairs of men
Which taken at the flood leads on to fortune;
Omitted, all the voyage of their life
Is bound in shallows and in miseries.
William Shakespeare, *Julius Caesar*, Act 4, Scene 3

'I imagine it is not surprising that an actor should choose William Shakespeare, England's greatest playwright, as his hero. His words express truths that are both universal and timeless and speak to people as much now as when first written. Although the words chosen have a specific context in the play, their message is still as relevant as ever. The need to recognize and seize an opportunity when it arises is surely something we all need to be aware of.'

Albert Einstein

(1879–1955)

$E = mc^2$

I know not with what weapons World War III will be fought, but World War IV will be fought with sticks and stones.

Attributed to Einstein

'I first became interested in Einstein when I was 17 before going to university to study astrophysics. At first I was interested in his work in theoretical physics, but the more I read about him, the more I became interested in the man.

His contributions to science include the theories of Special Relativity, General Relativity and his famous theory, Mass-Energy Equivalence ($E = mc^2$), yet he was revered not only for his immense leaps forward in theoretical physics. His views on philosophy, politics, religion, civil rights and the fate of humankind brought him an audience far beyond the scientific community. For all of this, *Time* magazine named him "Person of the Century" in 1999.

In 1939 many scientists feared that Germany might develop an atomic bomb, and Einstein, whose groundwork on physics had opened the way for the development of nuclear fission, was persuaded to sign a letter to the US President urging the United States to develop its own bomb. However, Einstein later expressed regret to Roosevelt about the letter and urged him not to pursue a nuclear weapons monopoly, but instead to equip the United Nations with them as a deterrent against conflict.'

Lt Col. Jeffery Williams
Retired Canadian army officer and author

❦

Lieutenant-General Sir Julian Byng
(1862–1935)

My great-uncle was shot for running away from Minorca. I was given a decoration for running away from Gallipoli. Now which is right, because surely they cannot both be?

Lieutenant-General Sir Julian Byng

'Following the desperate Ypres battles of 1914–15, Julian Byng was sent from the Western Front to Gallipoli to revive a failing enterprise, but instead, in the face of Kitchener's and Churchill's opposition, called for it to be abandoned. He then planned one of the most successful withdrawals in the history of war. In recognition, he was knighted. However, his great uncle, Admiral John Byng, though not its most distinguished member, is the best remembered of his family, for his name is coupled with Voltaire's sarcastic quip that in England they sometimes shoot an admiral "pour encourager les autres".

Field Marshal Viscount Byng of Vimy did not fit into the conventional mould, either in the Army, as Governor-General of Canada or as Commissioner of the Metropolitan Police. His life was suffused with a sense of humour and realism. He expected and was given the best by the best. Churchill, who admired him greatly and had been his "galloper" in the South African Light Horse during the Boer War, said, "No one ever cursed me as heartily as Bungo did in the Light Horse Days".

JESSICA ROXBURGH
Aged 8, Ash School, Somerset

The Policeman

Taking bad people away and putting them in jail,
Chasing them when they won't stop.
Fearless when he is up against it,
Saving the world for us to feel safe.

Jessica Roxburgh

THE MOST REVD AND RT HON. DR ROWAN WILLIAMS
Archbishop of Canterbury

St Augustine of Hippo
(354–430)

Lord our God, may we set our hope under the shadow of your wings. Protect us, carry us along. You will carry us when we are little, you will still be carrying us when our hairs are grey. When you are there in our weakness, then it is strong; when our strength is ours alone, it is nothing but weakness. What is good for us is always alive in you; and it is because we turn away from this that we are turned inside out. Lord, may we learn to turn back to you so that we may not be overturned for ever; because our good is always alive in you, without any falling or failing. What is good for us is nothing but you yourself – and so we need have no fears that when we return home we shall find only a ruin because we were so long away. Nothing touches our home, even when we are absent: that home of ours is your eternal life.

St Augustine, from Confessions, Book IV, Chapter xvi.5

'St Augustine of Hippo is perhaps the Christian thinker and bishop whom I most admire and most often quote.'

JEAN WILMSHURST

Teacher/tutor

Charles Dickens

(1812–70)

Mr Podsnap settled that whatever he put behind him he put out of existence . . . Mr Podsnap had even acquired a peculiar flourish of his right arm in often clearing the world of its most difficult problems, by sweeping them behind him.

From *Our Mutual Friend*, Chapter 11

I only know two sorts of boys, Mealy boys, and beef-faced boys.

From *Oliver Twist*, Chapter 14

'Charles Dickens was a great story teller and actor as well as writer, creating iconic characters which people remember and quote even if they have not read the book themselves. He sparked social reform by bringing the plight of the poor and the existing horrific regimes to public attention.'

REBECCA WILMSHURST

Executive Producer of BBC Radio Drama

Walter de la Mare

(1873–1956)

Fare Well

Look thy last on all things lovely,
Every hour. Let no night
Seal thy sense in deathly slumber
Till to delight
Thou have paid thy utmost blessing;

Since that all things thou wouldst praise
Beauty took from those who loved them
In other days.

Last verse of 'Fare Well'

'Walter de la Mare's reflections on life have, since childhood, fascinated and inspired me. His innate sense of awe and wonder is never more simply nor more powerfully expressed than at the close of "Fare Well" published in – of all years – 1918. His words echo Keats' enigmatic "Beauty is truth, truth beauty – that is all ye know on earth, and all ye need to know". For me, they are a reminder that all things that delight and inspire us now owe the intensity of their very loveliness to the strength of love and delight that others took in them in lives past. It is a legacy to pass from one generation to another – and I find in that a sense of enduring comfort and hope.'

The Revd John Witheridge

Headmaster of Charterhouse

Revd Dr Thomas Arnold

(1795–1842)

It is much pleasanter to think of evils which you may yourself hope to relieve, than those with regard to which you can give nothing but vain wishes and opinions.

Revd Dr Thomas Arnold

'Dr Arnold is perhaps the most famous of all headmasters. He was Headmaster of Rugby from 1828 to 1842 when he died in office, aged 47. During those 14 years he reformed the school by providing pastoral care, broadening the curriculum and putting the Christian faith firmly at the heart of the school. He inspired a generation of headmasters who spread his ideas and convictions.'

Grandpa Billy Rap

Grandpa Billy is the best,
He eats so fast he can't digest.

I like him because he's so cool,
He even has a swimming pool.

When it's time to go to bed,
Grandpa lets me stay up instead.

Grandpa tells funny jokes,
So come around, old folks.

He is more fun than the rest;
That's why Grandpa Billy's the BEST!

Benjamin Warman

ANNE WOOD

Television producer and creator of *Teletubbies*

Janusz Korczak

(1878–1942?)

When I approach a child I have two feelings. Appreciation for what he is today. And respect for what he can become.

The child's thinking is neither more limited nor inferior to that of an adult. It is different. The child thinks with feelings and not with the intellect. That is why communication is so complicated. And speaking with children is a difficult art.

It isn't what you play that is important – it is how you play. And what you think and feel when you are playing that matters. You can play intelligently with a doll. And you can play a foolish game of chess. You can use a great deal of imagination and be totally absorbed in playing at being a policeman, a train driver, or a cowboy. And you can read superficially and without interest.

Janusz Korczak

'Korczak, the great Polish educator, stayed with his orphanage for Jewish children in the Warsaw Ghetto and went with 200 children to the death camp Treblinka on 6 August 1942. It always touches me deeply that on their final walk to the railway tracks that carried them away, he encouraged the children each to take with them a special thing that they loved so much and to march bravely behind their own specially designed flag – green with white blossom on one side, and the blue star of David on the other. I could have chosen Korczak because of his undoubted bravery. He had opportunities to leave Warsaw, but chose to stay. But, more than this, above everything, his belief in children and the power of imaginative thinking makes him my hero. There are so many quotations that are deceptively simple, but carry with them the feeling of experience, so I have chosen those which I have found meaningful in my own work.'

❡ Korczak also observed that 'each person carries an entire world within himself. Everything exists twice – once the way it is; and the other, the way he perceives it with his own eyes and feelings'.

VIRGINIA WOODERSON

English teacher in Tuscany

Mark Antony

I am dying, Egypt dying; only
I hear importune death awhile, until
Of many thousand kisses the poor last
I lay upon thy lips.

William Shakespeare, *Antony and Cleopatra*, Act IV, Scene xv

'Antony seems to epitomize the Elizabethan ideal of the heroic soldier-poet. He is a brave warrior and adventurer. A superb orator, he sways the crowds after Caesar's assassination. He is sensitive to nature. But in the tragic Greek tradition he is fatally flawed. Shakespeare shows us with his great mastery how Antony's life unravels in the grip of uncontrollable passion.'

Dr C. J. Wright

Formerly Keeper of Manuscripts, British Library

The Heroes of the Light Brigade

(1854)

Fancy they sent us (by whose order it has not yet transpired although I heard Nolan most distinctly say 'Lord Raglan orders you to charge the enemy & take those guns') to advance half a mile along a narrow valley with 8 guns on a hill on the left, 2 columns of Infantry, 4 guns on the right, 9 guns in front, with about 3,000 Cavalry to protect them and no support. We were half down before we reached the guns but the men behaved like men and never wavered an inch, Grape & Shells cutting them to pieces. We drove them 500 yds from the guns & if there had been a support to walk them off all might have been taken. They cut in every direction, we had to fight our way back too through 2 Regiments of lancers who came on our rear – never was such murder ordered. We [the 13th] went 110 into it and lost 78 horses killed, 10 wounded, 7 officers horses' killed, 46 men killed, missing and wounded. However poor Howard fell in as they say about the most daring charge ever seen. The Light Brigade are half gone.

Captain Soame Jenyns of the 13th Light Dragoons

'On 25 October 1854, in the early stages of the Crimean War, nearly 700 British cavalry attacked the Russian guns at the head of a valley north of the British base at Balaklava. Due to confused orders, they were the wrong guns in the wrong valley. The manoeuvre was executed with supreme daring but, in the absence of support, lacked any military purpose. Ever since, the Charge of the Light Brigade has symbolized the conflicting emotions which war conjures up. Horror at the futility of the carnage mingles with admiration for the bravery of the officers and men involved. Their heroism was all the greater because it was obvious to those who took part that what they had been ordered to do made no sense. This letter, now in the British Library and written from Balaklava only two days after the battle by one of the stunned survivors, Captain Soame Jenyns of the 13th Light Dragoons, displays the sense of disbelief together with pride at what had been endured which captured the imagination of the nation.

It seems to me to conjure up something of the context of heroism and the questions it raises.'

ROY YOUDALE

Basket maker

Morihei Ueshiba

(1883–1969)

Contemplate the workings of this world, listen to the words of the wise, and take all that is good as your own. With this as your base, open your own door to truth. Do not overlook the truth that is right before you. Study how water flows in a valley stream, smoothly and freely between the rocks. Also learn from holy books and wise people. Everything – even mountains, rivers, plants, and trees – should be your teacher.

Morihei Ueshiba, founder of the Japanese art of Aikido

'I have been a student of Ki Aikido for some 16 years, and it has changed my life for the better in so many ways. Morihei Ueshiba's great gift to humanity was to turn the martial arts tradition of Japan into an art for self-development and peace, rather than for fighting. The art of Ki Aikido develops co-ordination of mind and body, calmness and relaxation through non-aggressive physical exercises. Ki means "life force". Aikido means "way of life to find harmony with nature"'.

SIR COLVILLE YOUNG
Governor of Belize

George Washington

(1732–99)

The study of agriculture should be a part of every man's education.

Attributed to George Washington

'I often quote this when talking to politicians, educationalists and other groups. I cannot verify the details of the attribution, but it is certainly as wise today as it was in Washington's day.'

¶ Although one of its smallest countries, Belize holds some of the world's most precious unspoilt environments, in particular its tropical forests and the barrier reef which is a World Heritage Site.

There is sometimes confusion with George Washington Carver, born a slave in the nineteenth century, who became a great agriculturist, but the quote is more confidently attributed to George Washington, the American President.

Abraham Lincoln

(1809–65)

We here highly resolve that the dead shall not have died in vain, that this nation, under God, shall have a new birth of freedom; and that government of the people, by the people, and for the people, shall not perish from the earth.

Abraham Lincoln, from the address at the dedication of the
National Cemetery, Gettysburg, 19 November 1863

'More than anyone else I can think of, he combined the highest possible idealism with an extremely practical and down-to-earth approach to the political problems of the day.'

Index of Contributors

Index of Heroes and Holy People

Acknowledgements

Every effort has been made to locate copyright holders, although in a small number of cases this has proved impossible. We are grateful for permission to reprint the following copyright material.

'With Christ death is transcended' by The Rt. Revd George Bell is used by permission Pearson Education Ltd.

Extracts from Swami Chinmayananda's 'Vedanta Through Letters' is used by permission of Central Chinmaya Mission Trust, Mumbai.

Quotation from Nikos Kazanzakis' 'The Odyssey, A Modern Sequel', translated by Kimon Friar is used by permission of Kazantzakis Publications, Greece.

Quotation from Colin Powell from 'My American Journey' (Random House). Used by permission.

Quotation from 'Albert Prince Consort' by Robert Rhodes James is used by permission of Lady Rhodes James.

Excerpt from 'The Only Speaker of his Tongue' by David Malouf is used by permission of the author.

Extract from p.347 from 'New Grove Dictionary of Music, 2e' edited by Stanley Sadie, which has been included in the insertion on Ralph Vaughan-Williams from W. H. Mellers, 'Music and Society', 1946 revised 1950 published by Dobson, London (1946) & Roy Publishers, New York (1950). Used by permission of Oxford University Press.

Extracts from the Authorized Version of the Bible (The King James Bible), the rights in which are vested in the Crown, are reproduced by permission of the Crown's Patentee, Cambridge University Press.

Extracts from Violette Szabo are used by permission of Tania Szabo.

Text from 'The Complete Works of Saint Teresa of Jesus', translated by E. Allison Peers is used by permission of the Continuum International Publishing Group Ltd.

Extracts from 'The Dalai Lama's Little Book of Wisdom' are reprinted by permission of HarperCollins Publishers Ltd, © (The Dalai Lama).

Extracts from Dietrich Bonhoeffer's 'Letters and papers from Prison' are reproduced by permission of SCM-Canterbury Press Ltd.

Extract from Virginia Woolf's 'A Room of One's Own' is reproduced by permission of The Society of Authors as the Literary Representative of the Estate of Virginia Woolf.

Quotation from Rabbi Hugo Gryn is used by permission of The Movement for Reform Judaism.

Extract from Douglas Adams' 'Dirk Gently's Holistic Detective Agency' is used by permission of Pan MacMillan.

Extracts from Julian of Norwich's '*The Revelations of Divine Love*', are used by permission of Darton, Longman and Todd Ltd.

Extracts from the speeches of John F. Kennedy are used by permission of The John F. Kennedy Presidential Library.

Extraxt from 'Four Discussions with W R Bion' by W R Bion is used by permission of Paterson Marsh Lit on behalf of the Estate of W R Bion.

Excerpt from Cautionary Verses by Hilaire Belloc (© Hilaire Belloc) is reproduced by permission of PFD on behalf of Hilaire Belloc.

Extract from 'Yes Minister' by Sir Antony Jay, published by BBC Books. Reprinted by permission of The Random House Group Ltd.

Extracts from 'The Lover Tells of the Rose in His Heart' and from 'An Acre of Grass by Grainne Yeats are used by permission of A.P. Watt Ltd on behalf of Grainne Yeats.

Extracts from 'Silent Spring' and 'The Sense of Wonder' are used by permission of Pollinger Ltd and The Estate of Rachel Carson.

Etract from 'the homily of Pope John XXIII for the canonization of St Martin de Porres is reprinted by permission of HarperCollins Publishers Ltd. © (Pope John XXIII)

Extract from Siegfried Sassoon's 'Soldier's Declaration' is used by permission of the Estate of Siegfried Sassoon.

Extracts from 'East Coker, V' from 'Four Quartets' by T. S. Eliot and 'Herman Melville' from 'Collected Poems' by W. H. Auden are used by permission Faber and Faber Ltd and © The Estates of T.S. Eliot and W. H. Auden.

Excerpts from 'Marguerite Porete: The Mirror of Simple Souls', translated by Ellen L. Babinsky. Copyright © 1993 by Ellen L Babinsky. Paulist Press, Inc., New York/Mahwah, N.J. Reprinted by permission of Paulist Press Inc. www.paulistpress.com

Extracts from 'The Spiritual World of Isaac of Syrian', Cistercian Studies

Series, number 175 are used by permission of Hilarion Alfayev, Cistercian Publications, Kalamazoo, Michigan 2000.

Extracts from 'The Matter of Wales' by Jan Morris are used by permission of Jan Morris.

Extract from Schweitzer is used by permission of Sonja and Robert Poteau.

Extract from Mahatma Gandhi is used by permission of Navajivan.

Scripture taken from the HOLY BIBLE, NEW INTERNATIONAL VERSION®. NIV®. Copyright © 1973, 1978, 1984 by International Bible Society. Used by permission of Zondervan. All rights reserved.

The poem 'To Julian Grenfell' is used by permission of A P Watt Ltd on behalf of The Trustees of the Maurice Baring Will Trust.

Quotations from T.C. Kingsmill Moore's 'A Man May Fish' are used by permission of Colin Smythe Limited.

Excerpts from 'The Dance' by Thorlad Coade reprinted by permission of HarperCollins Publishers Ltd © Thorald Coade.

Extract from 'Taken on Trust' by Terry Waite is reproduced by permission of Hodder and Stoughton Limited.

Excerpts from 'Francis and Clare: The Complete Works', translation and introduction by Regis J. Armstrong, O.F.M.C.A.P. and Ignatius C. Brady, O.F.M. Copyright © 1982 by Paulist Press. Paulist Press, Inc., New York/Mahwah, N.J. Reprinted by permission of Paulist Press Inc. www.paulistpress.com

'The Knowing Heart' written and translated by Kabir Helminski. Originally published by Threshold Books, Putney, Vermont. Used by permission.

'The Guest House' from 'The Illuminated Rumi' translated by Coleman Banks, published by Amber Lotus Press, is used by permission of Coleman Banks.

Extract from 'Speke' by Alexander Maitland originally published by Constable is used by permission.

'The Harper's Song for Inherkhawy' from 'Echoes of Egyptian Voices, translated by John L Foster. Copyright © University of Oklahoma Press. Used by permission.

Excerpt from 'Urbanus Magnus: the Book of the Civilized Man' by Daniel of Beccles is used by permission.

Excerpt from 'The Rule of St Benedict' translated by Abbott Justin McCann is used by permission of The Continuum International Publishing Group Ltd.

Excerpt from 'The Rebirth of Nature' by Rupert Sheldrake, published by Ebury is reprinted by permission of the Random House Group Ltd.

Excerpt from Matthew Fox's 'Illuminations of Hildegard of Bingen', Rochester

VT 0567 Copyright © 1985 Inner Traditions/Bear & Company www.bearandcompany.com. Used by permission.

'Where is He?' from 'Becoming Bamboo: Western and Eastern Explorations of the Meaning of Life' by Robert E. Carter is used by permission of McGill-Queen's University Press.

Extract from a speech by Winston Churchill is reproduced with permission of Curtis Brown Ltd, London on behalf of The Estate of Winston Churchill.

Excerpts from 'Cicero: Volume V', reproduced by permission of the publishers and the Trustees of the Loeb Classical Library, volume 342, translated by H. M. Hubbell, Cambridge, Mass.: Harvard University Press, Copyright © 1939 by the President and Fellows of Harvard College. The Loeb Classical Library ® is a registered trademark of the President and Fellows of Harvard College.

'Farewell' by Walter de la Mare is reproduced by permission of the Literary Trustees of Walter de la Mare and the Society of Authors.

Excerpts from 'Loving Every Child: Wisdom for Parents' by Janusz Korczak, Algonquin Books, Chapel Hill, NY., is reproduced by permission of Sandra Joseph.

Excerpt from 'The Art of Peace', by Morihei Ueshiba; Translated by John Stevens copyright © 2002 by John Stevens. Reprinted by arrangement with Shambhala Publications Inc., Boston, MA. www.shambhala.com.

Excerpt from 'The Way of the Bodhisattva' by Shantideva, translated by the Padmakara Translation Group, revised Edition, copyright © 1997, 2006 by the Padmakara Translation Group. Reprinted by arrangement with Shambhala Publications Inc., www.shambhala.com.

Excerpt from 'Thomas Sankara, un nouveau pouvoir' by Jean Ziegler and Jean-Phillipe Rapp, Editions Pierre-Marcel Favre, Switzerland, is used by permission.

Excerpts from 'The Last Days of Socrates' by Plato, translated with an introduction by Hugh Tredennick (Penguin Classics 1954, Third Edition 1969) Copyright © Hugh Tredennick, 1954, 1959, 1969, and from 'The Meaning of It All' by Richard Feynman (Penguin Books 1998), copyright © Richard Feynman 1998, are used by permission of the Penguin Group (UK).

Excerpt from 'Scivias (Know the Ways of the Lord)' Vol 3, Ch 13, in Davis (ed.) 'Hildegard of Bingen Anthology', SPCK 1990, is used by permission of SPCK.

Extract from Harley Granville Barker, Preface to 'Cymbeline', (1993, Nick Hern Books, London www.nickhernbooks.co.uk) is used by permission.

Extract from the poem 'Christmas' in 'Travellers' by George Mackay Brown is used by permission of John Murray (Publishers) Ltd.

Excerpts from 'Revelations of Divine Love' by Julian of Norwich, translated by Elizabeth Spearing, introduction and notes by A. C. Spearing (Penguin Classics, 1998). Translation copyright © Elizabeth Spearing, 1998. Introduction and notes copyright © A. C. Spearing, 1998 is used by permission of the Penguin Group (UK).

Extract from 'A History of England' by Andre Maurois, copyright © Andre Maurois 1937, is reproduced with permission of Curtis Brown Group Ltd, London.

Excerpts from the poem 'Reassessment' from 'Prayers and Poems' by Monica Furlong is reproduced by permission of SPCK.

Excerpts from 'Process and reality' by Alfred North Whitehead, Corrected Edition, edited by David ray Griffin and Donald W. Sherburne. Copyright © 1929 by Macmillan Publishing Company. Copyright renewed 1957 by Evelyn Whitehead. Copyright © 1978 by The Free Press. Used by permission of The Free Press, a Division of Simon & Schuster, Inc.

Nelson Mandela quotation copyright © Nelson Mandela. Reproduced from 'Long Walk to Freedom' by Nelson Mandela by kind permission of Little, Brown Book Group.

Excerpts from 'One Jesuit's Spirituality Journey' by Pedro Arrupe used by permission: © The Institute of Jesuit Sources, St. Louis, MO. All rights reserved.

Extract from 'John Berger is wrong to boycott Israel' by Michael Berkeley (first published in The Guardian in 2006): Copyright © 2006 Michael Berkeley. Reproduced by permission of the author c/o Rogers, Coleridge & White Ltd., 20 Powis Mews, London W11 1JN.

Scripture taken from the New King James Version ®. Copyright © 1982 by Thomas Nelson, Inc. Used by permission.

Extract from 'Revelation of Divine Love' by Clifton Wolters is used by permission of John Wolters.

Extracts from 'Perseus in the Wind' by Freya Stark, copyright © 1948 and 'The Valleys of the Assassins' by Freya Stark, copyright 1934 are used by kind permission of John Murray (Publishers) Ltd.

Extracts by Hildegard of Bingen are used by permission of Corpus Christianorum.

Thank you to Python & Peter for their advice on the Sir Peter Ustinov quotation.